A Clearer View

New Insights Into the Sudbury School Model
The Thirtieth Anniversary Lectures

Daniel Greenberg

The Sudbury Valley School Press

Copyright © 2000 by The Sudbury Valley School Press
2 Winch Street, Framingham, MA 01701

ISBN #1-888947-22-5

Contents

Foreword   1

The Meaning of Play   3

Conversation: The Staple Ingredient   31

What *is* the Role of Parents   49

The Significance of the Democratic Model   72

Developing Each Child's Unique Destiny   92

Why the School Doesn't Work for Everyone   117

Foreword

During the school year 1998-99, Sudbury Valley School celebrated its thirtieth anniversary. One of the activities scheduled was a series of six lectures I presented as a retrospective, dealing with some fundamental questions that have occupied us over the years. I tried to convey some notion of how my thinking about these questions has developed with time. Audio-tapes of the lectures are available from The Sudbury Valley School Press. The present book is an edited version of the transcripts of these tapes. I tried to retain the flavor of an oral presentation, while eliminating some of the awkwardness that always accompanies a transcription from lecture to print.

Daniel Greenberg
January, 2000

The Meaning of Play

Back in 1965, a small group of us started discussing a set of ideas about education and schooling. That was when we began to become self-conscious of the fact that rather than just being critics, we were actually beginning to formulate some kind of philosophy of education. When we go back and read the papers that we wrote in '65-'67, we find that some of them have worn well with time, but many of the areas to which we are now sensitive were completely unexplored. The beauty of Sudbury Valley is that, over the years, there have been a tremendous number of people who have provided input into the thinking about the school. If you want some idea of what I'm talking about, you can just look in the sewing room at the collection of bound volumes of the Sudbury Valley School *Newsletter* (now called *Journal*) from the start in 1971. By now hundreds of essays have been written over the years by a great many people, refining the ideas that underlie the school.

We've had a lot of opportunities to re-think our ideas. We give talks to university groups, to organizations, to conferences, and each time we prepare to do such a thing, we have to reexamine what we're saying in light of our most current thinking. This makes change and development the order of the day in every area.

There is another major arena in which there has been a great deal of refinement of thinking about the school's philosophy and practice – the School Meeting. There, through the mundane discussion of everyday affairs, just about every aspect of the school's philosophy gets a thorough going-over at one time or another. It really never ceases to amaze me – and I know this is true of everybody else who has been part of the school – that here we are, thirty years later, and we still have School Meetings in which the debates are fresh; not always pleasant, but fresh, in which issues that one thinks had been settled long ago, are raised again, reexamined, and sometimes recast.

In this series of talks, I have picked six areas that I consider important to the school, in which my own thinking has undergone a great deal of change and development over the years. Tonight's subject is "The Meaning of Play".

Initially, play had a bad rap as a concept in the educational world. It was looked down on, considered not serious. That's reflected in the dictionary definition: "To occupy oneself in amusement, sport or other recreation. To act in jest or sport." You can see that's clearly something a serious educator would say has no place in education. It's almost antithetical to education. Education is something serious. Education is learning. It's the acquisition of knowledge, not to be confused with "fun", "jest", "recreation", "sport", etc.

So for a long time play, from an educator's point of view, just didn't belong. I remember growing up in schools that had a fifteen minute recess in the morning and another in the afternoon. We went to school from 9:00AM to 3:00PM, and recess was the only time we played. It was very clear that during recess we were being given a chance to do what we *didn't do* the rest of the time!

The problem for educators was that children seemed to like to play. In fact, people of all ages seem to like to play. Little kids like to play, as do older kids, and even teachers! Everybody likes to play. It plagues the educational system, the system is forever battling against this natural drive to engage in play, a tendency that the unruly clients of the system seem unable to overcome.

The natural attraction people have to play was a central preoccupation of educational reformers in the post-World-War-II era. That was a time when thinking people started reexamining education, and for good reason. It didn't take a great deal of insight to realize that something was off kilter, because the most sophisticated people in the world, from the European point of view – the people with the highest level of education and cultural refinement – had been engaged by 1945 in some thirty years of continuous mutual slaughter, filled with hatred and every brutality that could be conceived. That the most advanced nations educationally should coincide with the most brutal, led everybody who was interested in education to realize that something fundamental had to be reexamined. That was the golden age of educational reform and its momentum has carried forth to this day.

One of the trends in educational reform was to seize upon this universal desire of people to play, and to incorporate it somehow into schooling. The idea that learning should be fun, that learning and fun should be combined, that somehow joy should be insinuated into the learning process, was a result of this recognition that something had to change, and that one place to start was with the universal desire to play. The

Progressive School movement, in the '20s and '30s, first promulgated this idea, and after the War it really picked up steam. The idea was basically simple: stick to the original concept of what schooling is about, but incorporate "recreation" as a seduction. The old Hebrew day schools used to be blunt and up-front. They had parents send their kids to school the first day with honey on their chalkboards. There the bribe was open. You go to school, you get sweets. You do well, you get sweets. In the modern incarnation, the bribes were more sophisticated, and it was hoped that people wouldn't notice that the fundamental agenda hadn't changed.

How strong this movement is can be seen from the huge flap in Massachusetts just a short while ago. John Silber, the state's famous and often notorious education czar, engaged in a tremendous battle with a class of elementary school children who had the gall to write him on the theme of learning as fun. He erupted in a severe reply which was widely publicized, to the effect that people have it all wrong. According to Silber, learning isn't supposed to be fun! It's supposed to be strictly serious, and the schoolchildren who wrote him were admonished to straighten out their act and get the fun out of it. *Now*, if not sooner!

When Sudbury Valley opened, we knew, of course, as did everybody else, that kids would play a lot if they were allowed to be free, if they didn't have any externally-imposed agenda. We knew that if you really let kids control their own time, they would engage in a lot of play. We accepted that, but we were to a certain extent affected in our thinking by the prevailing notions at that time. We said, "It's okay that they play," not because learning is fun, but because *play itself is educational.* Play may be recreation and fun, but it fulfills "legitimate" educational goals, such as the development of certain motor skills, social skills, and other useful talents. Perhaps they'll play all day, but that's okay because it enhances certain aspects of their education.

Not surprisingly, we encountered a lot of objection from some parents in the school and from a lot of people who came to interview or consider sending their kids to the school, because they had the same problem that Silber had. Their attitude was: "You may say that play is okay and that it enhances certain educational goals, but *life isn't fun.* And if kids don't learn that life isn't fun early on, they're not being prepared for the world. The world is full of hard knocks, and presumably the consequence of that view is that the best way to raise kids is to give them a lot of hard knocks; or at least not to let them play."

What I want to focus on today is how our understanding of play deepened, because it's very different from where we started. Let me open with the question, "What is play, really?" With all due respect to the editors of the *American Heritage Dictionary*, I think they missed the essence of play completely. I think that the essence of play is the *indeterminate portion of the activity*. Play is an activity that has a significant part of it not determined, free from prior boundaries. If you examine the way the word "play" is used in its broadest sense in our language, you'll see that it is applied over and over again to activities where everything isn't specified, where you're not in a rigid box, where there's an unknown piece. That, of course, includes joy and entertainment, but it includes things like "playing with ideas". It includes even such a thing as "giving a little play" in a rope. Whenever something isn't taut, there's a little "play" in it. That's a good image to keep. When it's not fixed, when it's not rigid, you're involved in an activity that has an element of play.

As I see it, there are two major kinds of play. One I'll call "an undetermined activity within a very broad framework" – "free play", we might call it. For example, kids get together and say, "Let's play 'house'." They've got a broad framework. They're not playing "horse", they're not playing "fishing", and they're not playing "train". They're playing "house". So the overall general framework is set. But within that, at the outset, it's open-ended. We make it up as we go along. Will there be a father and a mother? Will there be uncles, grandchildren? A whole gamut of things is left open at the beginning. Or a more sophisticated example – for somebody like Jules Verne – let's play "invent a submarine". "Let's design an underwater vehicle". That's all we know about it, but it's a broad framework.

I've been at Sudbury Valley School for thirty years and still I was absolutely floored the other day by two girls who are well into their teens, coming up to me all excited and showing me a vehicle that they had designed. They had played "let's invent" and they had drawings and plans. They had come up with this broad idea and they sat down and talked about it. They drew, they changed their drawings, and they modified their plan. To tell you the truth, I was shocked, because I had never encountered this directly in somebody that age in the school. I've encountered it with older people for whom it's okay, at $80,000 a year or so, to play "let's invent a submarine". I've encountered it in little kids. But never directly with that age group, and it only hit me then that this must be going on all the time with people that age. It's just that you're self-conscious about it in your teens. It looks childish and you're not being paid a high salary to do it, so you keep it to yourself.

The second kind of play is undetermined activity within a narrow framework. That's an activity where there are a lot of boundaries, but there's still a good deal of freedom of action within them – for example, any game with rules. "Let's play Monopoly." What's the "play" in Monopoly? There are all these rules. You can't just do what you want. You have to roll the dice, move the pieces this way, go to jail, get out of jail, and all that. But a lot is not determined. Part of it by the throw of the dice. Part of it by how you strategize.

Or consider, "Let's play computer games." That seems like an especially highly determined environment, at first sight. It's so determined that people who don't know very much about computer games always claim it's mind numbing, because they focus on the images on the computer screen and the repetitiousness that they see in those images. They consider the activity to be robot-like, and they miss the "play" in it, the undetermined part.

It's obvious we can't always sharply distinguish an undetermined activity within a broad framework from one within a narrow framework, because there's every kind of degree in between. For example, in every case of play, whether it's within a broad framework or a narrow framework, there are rules. Play and rules are not incompatible with each other. On the contrary, they're always found together. There are always "rules of the game". The question is, how many rules there are. Some of the rules are man made, some are made by nature. If you want to play at inventing a submarine, you've got the properties of water that you have to deal with. What makes it play is that, no matter how many rules, no matter how broad or narrow the framework, there's an indeterminate part of the activity that allows for a lot of freedom of action.

Seeing play in this light helps explain why play is always closely linked to the concept of curiosity, to which we at Sudbury Valley were very sensitive from the beginning. Curiosity is the innate drive that people have to explore the unknown – in other words, *to explore the, as yet, undetermined.* Inherent in the exploration of the unknown is an indeterminate activity. *Curiosity drives play, and play feeds on curiosity.* They're very closely interlinked. We've frequently quoted Aristotle's statement, made some 2,000 years ago, that human beings are by nature curious. But what we didn't appreciate until much later is that being naturally curious links closely to the idea of play. Curiosity implies the desire to play, because they both involve indeterminateness.

It's an observed fact that play is universal. It's freely chosen by people of all ages. People enjoy it.

People devote enormous amounts of energy to it. They focus on it. They don't complain about the amount of effort they put into it. Worth noting in this connection is an observation that many of us have made in this school when dealing with so-called "attention-deficit disorders". Over and over again with children who supposedly are lacking ability to pay attention to something for an extended period, if you ask their parents whether they play, the answer is invariably, "Oh, yes. They can play for hours." They can carve wood, play computer games, write, do all sorts of play activities, for hours on end. But they can't pay attention to their school work. The point is that focusing is a side effect of play. Play is so engrossing, so involving, it absorbs your whole personality, your whole psyche. Only if I encounter a child who is unable to carry out the activity of play with focus and with energy, do I know that I've encountered a situation that is potentially a serious problem from a health point of view.

What makes play so central to the human race? What is its evolutionary function? My contention is that the survival and enhancement of the human species is centrally linked to play. Here's how I see it: human beings as a species are unique, with respect to the extent to which they have a pro-active interaction with the environment. Human beings have the ability to interact with the environment in a way that is aggressively interactive – to manipulate the environment, understand it, create models of the environment, modify it, and have it feed back information to them. One of the ways humans interact with the environment is by seeking to affect conditions in a way that will enhance human welfare.

So, it's part of human nature – the pro-active interaction with the environment – to be able to seek ways to change the environment through the exploration of the unknown. And the way mankind progresses is by looking for new, *as yet undetermined*, factors, taking advantage of them, developing them, bringing them within the realm of human knowledge, and then going on from there to new unknowns.

There is no change in condition without innovation. That's a tautology. There are, again, not surprisingly, two kinds of innovation that progress humanity. One is open-ended innovation, free-form invention, and the other is innovation within a more determinate framework.

Let's look first at open-ended innovation within a broad domain. An example is the invention of the microscope. Huyghens was an optician. He was a highly skilled craftsman. He was on the cutting edge of optics, and lenses, etc. So he had the broad framework of optics, of light, and related fields. He was "playing" with these, in the deepest sense of the term. It was an accident, in a sense, that he discovered that a certain configuration of lenses gave incredible enlargements – an accident in the sense that he didn't expect it to happen before he did it. There was nothing in the theory of optics at the time that led him to believe that this would occur. That's what I mean by open-ended innovation. He had a broad framework within which he was working. But his curiosity, his play, his experimentation led him to a point where he could make something that could see very small objects.

To appreciate this, I recommend to you to try to invent the microscope. I say this half-jokingly because I taught college physics for many years, and one thing that students do in most introductory physics labs is build a microscope. You give the kids lenses and you say, "Make a microscope"; of course, there's a lab manual that tells them what to do. Even so, it's very, very difficult. You can't see anything most of the time. It doesn't work unless they're just the right kinds of lenses, the right kinds of distances and the image that you're looking at is just in the right place. The same is true of a telescope. Putting two lenses together is a really difficult game to play, a really difficult kind of invention.

Computers are another example of what I call open-ended innovation. The idea of a calculating machine goes back to the 19th century, but that's a far cry from the particular way computers are put together. Mathematicians in general are a breed unto themselves; they spend their entire lives playing. The people who invented the computer were playing with open-ended innovations, and they had no idea where they would lead. Today, it is hard to realize how far into the unknown they were probing. You can get a feel for it if you read the history of computers. After the first large computer had been put together (by large, I mean, LARGE; I mean a computer that took up much more room than the school's barn, most of it filled with radio tubes), people said to the Chairman of IBM, "This is a very interesting machine. Obviously it can do a lot. Do you envision a considerable market for this?" And he replied, "Not really. I can imagine four or five such machines being needed in the world." Even more remarkable is the story of the history of personal computers. The founder of Intel, the chip makers, was asked, "How come you guys didn't invent the personal computer? You had it in the palm of your hands." The chip is the computer, basically, for all intents and purposes. "You had the chip." And he answered, "We knew we had it, so we sat around and brainstormed about what a personal computer could be used for.

Nobody could think of any use except for collecting recipes. I said to my colleagues that I could not see my wife sitting in the kitchen with this gadget, filling out recipes. So we dropped it." I believe that story because it has the ring of truth. It's typical about open-ended innovation. It's so far out. It's extremely new. It's a leap. It doesn't fit anything.

My last example is the invention of electromagnetic waves, by James Clerk Maxwell. He devised formulas which predicted, among other things, that electromagnetic waves could travel through space at the speed of light. These formulas were published in the 1860's and nobody paid any attention. He was a very famous man. Everybody recognized him as a leading figure in physics. But the idea of the waves just sat there. It was over 25 years later that a German experimental physicist by the name of Hertz happened to wonder whether there actually might be phenomena like that. He figured out an easy way to find out. He set up a little experiment, guided by Maxwell's equations, that would create a spark at one place and cause an effect somewhere else. He plugged it in, started it, and it worked! So he published a paper which said that electromagnetic waves exist – and everybody went back to sleep. It didn't mean anything within the prevailing framework of physics at the time.

Let's look at the other kind of innovation, that occurs within a more determinate framework. We have a name for that in our culture. We call it "Research and Development" (R&D). A very interesting point was made a while ago in the *Economist* magazine. One of the editors wrote a little piece on R&D *vs* free-form invention. R&D has a bit of a bad rap, like computer games, like all play within a narrower framework. R&D is the stepson of "real" invention in the hierarchy of the cognitive world. Who are considered to be the geniuses? The inventors. What do second-rate people do? They do R&D. That little piece in the *Economist* pointed out that really significant advances, in terms of the human progress that I'm talking about, are always made in the R&D field. Great inventions, in and of themselves, have minimal impact on cultural progress. History books exalt them and talk about the great genius of inventors. But the impact on society, on human advancement, really comes from the genius of R&D because R&D focuses on innovating within the new framework which the invention created.

All microscopic biology came from Huyghens' invention. It's all R&D, a parade of people making one slide after another, cutting up samples and doing all sorts of seemingly repetitive and boring work, from which ultimately emerged all the discoveries and inventions that constitute cellular biology.

Electromagnetic waves were dormant until a fellow named Marconi, an R&D guy from Italy, actually used them to send messages across the Atlantic. After that, people grasped that this was a gigantic advance in human communication.

Of course, there's no sharp dividing line between the two kinds of innovation. The case of x-rays is an amusing example of the crossover when somebody doing R&D happens across an open-ended innovation. It's a wonderful story because Roentgen, the fellow who discovered x-rays, was probably one of the most boring physicists who ever lived. His field was viscosity and the way he spend his time was dropping little metal balls through tubes of liquid, watching how fast they dropped. I'm exaggerating, but that's about as exciting as it was. I don't want to go into details of the story but in his lab it so happened that he came across x-rays. In his own field, he wasn't an open-ended innovator, but he noticed this phenomenon, which I'm sure others before him had seen, and he became curious enough to "play" with it. In fact, he was so excited – this was the only exciting thing that ever happened in his life – that he locked himself into his lab for a week. He refused to let anybody in because he was afraid somebody would scoop him. He made them leave his food outside the door. After a week he published a paper and he was never heard from again, basically, because the second he published his paper, everybody who knew about the field he had stumbled onto leapt in and did their R&D and swept way ahead. But he's the discoverer; they're still called "Roentgen Rays" in Europe.

There is a close correspondence between the two kinds of innovation and the two kinds of play, because the two kinds of play are the progenitors of the two kinds of innovation. This doesn't mean that every open-ended play will create a cultural revolution of innovation, and it doesn't mean that every play within a narrower framework will lead to a great R&D development like the PC, but the two activities are closely related, by nature.

Aristotle, who was so clever in so many ways, intuitively recognized this. He understood the importance of undetermined activity for human progress. He called it "leisure", but he really meant the ability to perform activities that have no fixed bounds. Aristotle pointed out very simply that culture depended on leisure and that the extent to which the human race is able to enjoy leisure is the extent to which the human race is able to move beyond its confines and to advance.

The Greeks liked their leisure and they truly believed that leisure created culture. The best place you can see that is in their schools – for example, as pictured in Plato's dialogues. Read "The Symposium", one of the great philosophical pieces of all time. It's a discussion of great philosophical ideas and it takes place in a drunken orgy. Literally. An orgy in which the main theme was, can anyone drink more than Socrates? This was another way of proving what a great philosopher Socrates was! The point is that great thinking comes out of non-structured, open-ended play. The Greeks weren't embarrassed about it. They didn't have a hidden agenda. They didn't say, "We're playing, but as a side result we're getting motor skills." The leisure activity produced the culture and where there was no leisure, there was no advance of culture as far as the Greeks could see.[1]

---

[1] During the question-and-answer period following the talk, the following exchange took place:
  Q. I think some of the problem comes with the use of the word "leisure", because we define it as time that we can do whatever we want, like ski, or sail. But leisure, the way I see you using the word, can include working a twelve hour day. If, in fact, that's what you want to be doing. If you love writing pieces to market something, that's leisure time.
  D. That's right. It means anything not devoted to the absolute essential biological survival.
  Q. That's where we get into trouble because we're working x amount of hours to get this much leisure time and, in fact, the leisure could be built in all along the way in the work hours, if the mind is free and having a good time.
  D. That's the exact same problem I was referring to with the word "play," because play really means something much broader. Actually, it's work in the creative sense.

From this perspective, human history really has two major eras: All of history until now; and the post industrial age. During the first era, permission to play was only granted to a small, powerful elite. The reason for this is that the full efforts of the vast majority of the human race were required for survival work. The elite who could afford leisure usually maintained their special status by some kind of brute force; but since you can't rule the whole human race just by force, you have to use psychological mechanisms too. You have to convince the people they shouldn't want leisure. The denigration of play is part of this massive campaign against leisure. The thing to do is work. The thing to do is your "duty".

Why did 95% of the population accept this state of affairs for so long? History holds the answer. When society moved from hunter/gatherer to agricultural, much more changed than economic factors. All kinds of evolutionary behavior that the human race had developed to adapt to its initial hunter/gatherer situation had to undergo transformation as well. What enabled this to happen was the great material gains provided by the transition. In particular, people had more food than ever before. This provided a little surplus for an elite, which in turn led to substantial non-material gains – namely, the beginning of a broad-based culture. You have art, you have theatre, you have music, you have literature, you have advanced technology, you have accurate recorded history, you have a judicial system. The reason most of the population could accept their situation is that, overall, they gained more than they lost. How many people throughout the agricultural era got up and left the farms to go back to tribal life? You don't find people leaving the cities of Syria and Egypt *en masse* and saying, "Forget all this. Let's go back to the Sahara Desert or to the Central African jungle because life is much better there. We can be freer." They stayed put because, even though they didn't have the freedom and personal status that they had as hunter/gatherers, the gains were tremendous. It's a kind of cultural cost-benefit analysis: people tolerate a radically new state of affairs because on the whole they're better off than they were in the older state of affairs.

When you get the transition from an agricultural to an industrial society, you have the same kind of situation. You have another leap forward, more material gains and more cost. Instead of people being slaves to the land, they're slaves to the factory. They work longer hours, but they live better than ever before. Once again, how many people streamed out of cities to go back to farms? Why did people emigrate in the other direction? Because however miserable their urban lives were, the gains were worth the cost.

So for thousands of years, only a small fraction of the population was in a position to have the leisure to contribute to the growth of culture in any profound way. This situation was maintained because the rest of the population, overall, benefitted more than they paid. They were able to eat better, dress better, live better, and be healthier than ever before. From the vantage point of the 20th century, life in the 1700's may not look very appealing, but to somebody living then, life in Liverpool looked a lot better than life on the farm. And to somebody living in the year 3000 B.C., living in Babylon felt a lot better than living in the mountains of Kurdestan.

Now we're in the second great human era, the post industrial age. That era is defined by the invention of devices which replace all mechanical activity by electronically driven, semi-intelligent activity. It frees an ever-growing percentage of the human race from having to devote themselves to basic survival needs. A small fraction of the work that you do is required to satisfy your basic needs for food, clothing, and shelter. The age of leisure for everybody is at hand. We were brought up with the older concepts, with the remnants of the earlier era's way of thinking. Children growing up today, however, understand intuitively, if not cognitively, that the future belongs to leisure, and that the challenge of being an adult in the future is being able to use your leisure to the fullest extent of your potential, to be able to use every bit of your skill and innovative capability and creativity. Play is the centerpin of the future. It's not a side issue. It's the key to the future.[2]

---

[2]   During the question-and-answer period following the talk, the following exchange took place:

Q. I would like to be optimistic, but I'm a little concerned because I think one can see other points in recent history where we have had the same opportunity presented. I'm thinking, for instance, when we had the entry of women to the work force, it shouldn't take more than forty hours to feed a family. But, in fact what happened is it has taken sixty to eighty. The total amount of labor that it takes to feed a family is, in fact, going up. It doesn't seem to me that's because we're getting more stuff. Maybe I'm too young to realize how much more stuff we're getting, but it seems to me in large part that what's happening is that this economy is creating jobs that are not productive; that an awful lot of the work people are obliged to do in order to eat, is not work to produce the food that's eaten, not work to produce the clothes that are worn, but work, instead, to sell the food that is eaten, sell the clothes that are worn, basically changing the flow of capital from one set of hands to another without the actual creation of capital. So I have trouble being optimistic about a turnaround in the culture that enables people to be freed from unnecessary labor because, at least the way things have been going, the culture seems to be doing everything it can to make sure that everyone's got busy work.

D: You just described the turnaround! That, to me, is the most interesting facet of the turnaround, one that is perhaps hardest to recognize. The way I discovered that for myself was when I was thinking about housing. I guess this was about ten years ago, when one of the things that everybody was moaning about was that the American Dream was over, because it's too expensive to buy a house, etc. You don't hear quite as much about this today because of the housing turnaround. When I started thinking about that, I said to myself, "Wait a minute, what kind of house did I grow up in the 1930's and 1940's? A house in the year 1500 meant four mud walls and some kind of a grass roof and a mud floor and basically no furniture. Most everyone had a "house" then. A house in 1900 meant something else. In 1930, when my parents bought their house in a very nice suburb of Philadelphia, it was considered a nice, middle class house. Today, it couldn't be sold! The house of today is something entirely different.

What you're describing is exactly the turnaround. What people see as not producing "useful capital" is the production of *variety*. Let's back up for a minute. What is the problem for an entrepreneur, or any inventor? It's marketing his idea. I don't care whether you paint pictures, take photographs, build buildings, you can be the best in the world, if you cannot market yourself, if you can't get somebody else to be willing to part with cash for what you're doing, you might as well do something else. The whole point of marketing is to get your product, what you have done, what you have created, out there to enough people that somebody will want to pick it up. The turnaround happens in this age where you have so many new avenues of marketing, so much vaster communication ability than you had forty years ago. The reason people want all these things, the reason people are working so hard, is because there are just so many more interesting things out there to get. It's not because they're greedy. It's because the products are *interesting*. It's more aesthetically interesting to own pretty clothes. It's actually nice to have more than one pair of shoes.

There are so many ways to illustrate this new phenomenon. For example, consider the proliferation of magazines. When I was young, there were Life, Time, Fortune – just a handful. Today there's a magazine for everything: for bicyclists, for runners, for racketball, tennis, etc. More than one. And they're all lavishly illustrated and they all have lots of focused ads in them. Puritans look at all this and say, "This is a society of greed. It's not producing real things." It's ridiculous. This is a society in which imagination is running wild. And the fact that people want to work another ten hours a week, in order that they can buy these really neat interesting ideas that they come across, is a sign that they're more excited about life, in my view. Our society is bubbling with this excitement. But we're still slightly ashamed of it, because we've got this Puritan ethic boring down on us. So while we're all doing it, we're saying, "Oh, what a terrible thing. We've become so materialistic. We've worked so hard. We're not enjoying it anymore. We work twice as hard. We barely make it." But in fact, what we're really doing, when we're not thinking in those dark terms, is going to the mall to see what's new! That's the imagination working, not greed!

Just compare what's on the shelves in the supermarket today with what I went to a store to buy when I was a kid and there were no supermarkets! So what does food mean today? I have a friend who lived on next to nothing because he lived on food that would have been perfectly standard in 19th-century Ireland. He lived on boiled onions and boiled potatoes! And he did fine. His food budget was nil. If you want to live on potatoes and onions, you can live on very little. Same with a car. A car means something totally different from the tin Lizzie we owned in 1945. You couldn't even get a thing like that registered anymore. You can clothe yourself very nicely on very little money. But, it doesn't have the same excitement. It doesn't have the same meaning.

That's innovation. That's play. That's what it is to be human. That's what our 19-month old grandchild is doing all day. He's looking for new excitement in the house. There isn't a thing that we can keep in the house anymore. The house is a shambles because he wants to look at everything.

People are beginning to appreciate that free play is creative activity. Unfortunately, a lot of times when people write about play, they get caught up in trying to prove that it's OK by giving a quantitative measure to children's ability to play and be creative. They put children in laboratories and tell them to be creative in one way or another. I have nothing against that, except that it doesn't measure what we're talking about. It's inherently impossible to measure the benefit of leisure, because the essence of creativity is that it's indeterminate, while the essence of measurement is precisely that it *is* determinate. These two cannot coexist. The minute you circumscribe an activity enough to measure it, you've lost its true innovative value.

The nature of play within a narrow framework, and its connection to R&D, is a lot less appreciated. A sonnet is perfect example of what I'm talking about. A sonnet is a highly structured form of poetry, yet some of the greatest poetry has been written in sonnet form. The beauty of creativity here is the great artist's struggle to be innovative within this framework. That's the R&D challenge. We praise people who succeed in doing that. We call them great poets. If all the students in Sudbury Valley were sitting down and writing sonnets all day, everybody would be thrilled. Nobody would have a problem. We'd have a waiting list of a thousand people. "This is a school where people write sonnets." But tell people that there are children who sit and play computer games for five hours, and they're beginning to wonder whether they should let their kids enroll, or mix with other kids who do that. "Don't go to the barn! It's OK for you to go to school, but don't go to the barn." The challenge for us is to have people see that these are two aspects of the same thing. We're just not comfortable with certain activities, because we didn't grow up with them. Adults over thirty years old – I don't care how computer-literate they are – are not in the same place mentally as young kids relative to the creative potential of maneuvering within computer games. You've got to see it to understand it. Personally, I can't *feel* it, but I can *see* it. I can see it in the eyes of the people involved. I can see it in their conversation, in their interactions.

The basic point I'm trying to make is that giving children the freedom to play is giving them the freedom to explore the nature of the innovative process first-hand. To give that freedom is the most direct way to provide an environment in which their lifelong useful adult activities will be foreshadowed, as they enter the era of innovation, leisure, and creativity.

That leads to a final observation. As children grow older in the school, their play naturally progresses to modalities that are more appropriate to adulthood. This is a natural process. It's a matter of continuity. It's the same activity, just engaged in a few years later. And all of the characteristics of play – the joy, the focus, the concentration continue into adulthood.

As to the question, "Why is play fun?", the answer is simply that this guarantees that the human race will go on doing it. Otherwise, why bother doing it? It's like sex. It's just as central. Curbing play is just like enforcing celibacy.

Conversation: the Staple Ingredient

The sub-title was carefully chosen to represent the status I think conversation has relative to the entire process of learning and living.

This is a retrospective series of talks about what we've learned over the thirty years, and I find it rather interesting to note how thoroughly we missed this subject in the early years. In our early literature, there is hardly a mention of conversation. We talked a lot about how we expected children to play a lot, and play they did, from day one. They also talked a lot from day one, but we didn't really understand what was going on. We just casually assumed that talking was one of those things you do, like breathing and eating. The significance of conversation and its centrality really took a long time to grow on us during the years. It's only recently that we have even noticed that conversation is something ubiquitous at school, that it's a major activity for children of all ages and the primary activity for teenagers.

When you finally notice a phenomenon like that in a school such as ours, where children are free to do as they please, you are bound to ask, "Why? Why is conversation an activity that is so passionately engrossing?" An incident that focused it all for me was a little scene that I saw from the second floor window one day a few years ago. I saw three rather young girls walking down from the parking lot on the road. They must have been about seven years old. As they were walking down, they were engaged in an obviously intense conversation. I couldn't hear a word. But it *looked* exactly as if it were three adults walking down. These were three little girls and they looked completely adult, walking and talking. That little scene made the final transition for me; I realized that what they were doing was as important to them, as meaningful to them, as it is to adults who are engaged in the same kind of conversation.

The challenge for me then became to understand why, and not only to understand why but to get some handle on what it is they talk about. That's what I plan to explore tonight because I think we've gained a lot of insight into that over these decades.

Let's start with a definition of conversation, so that we know what we're discussing. A conversation is a verbal exchange between one person and one or more others. Its most common form is oral, but there are other forms of conversation. There's written conversation through mail. Now, in the information age, there's e-mail, which is that beautiful crossover between oral conversation and formal mail, where you can communicate rather quickly back and forth, but not so quickly that you have to be on your toes and respond on the spot. There's that interesting form of conversation with yourself, when you're talking things over with yourself – usually silently, using words in your mind.

Conversation is a form of interpersonal communication. There are other forms of communication between people, but conversation is specifically a *verbal* form. It depends on an exchange of words. Its main function is to acquire information, and to affect the environment via words. For example, when we use words to get somebody to do something for us, that's using words to affect the environment. The key element here is the *word*. To get a real handle on what conversation is, we have to understand what words are, what language is.

We're going to enter now into a rather complex domain. Many philosophers have written about language. It's a difficult subject and it's still very much under study and investigation. Let me give my perspective on it.

Human beings, like every other animal, as part of their survival needs have to comprehend the world. The way living beings comprehend the world by developing what I call "models of reality". They develop a picture in their minds of what the reality surrounding them is. Each and every one of us has an individual model of reality. And just as important as having a model of reality, which is a picture, each one of us develops a mode of interacting with our environment, by which we affect the environment, gain things from the environment, and use our senses to interact with the environment. So, there's both the static picture that we have – the model – and also the mode of creating and refining the model. I needed a shorthand to describe this dual function that each of us has, that's uniquely ours – our model of reality, which is ever-changing, and our mode of interacting with reality; I've called it our "modor". The modor designates the totality of mechanisms by which a person makes sense out of life. This includes all the instrumentalities of interaction with the environment (for example, those mediated by the senses and all the ways by which the inputs into the person's system get processed), and all the representations people make of the world around them, conscious and unconscious, cognitive and emotional.

The modor is something very personal. It's our unique way of seeing the world and our way of viewing and interacting with the world. Each person, from birth on, develops their own specific modor, which is constantly changing, constantly affected by their life experiences.

What evolution has given humans is one specific additional tool that, as far as we know, no other animal has for building modors, and that is the ability to create symbols for our thoughts. A word is a discrete entity, a shorthand, which we use all the time in constructing and developing our modors.

A word is a symbol that has a host of things that it refers to in our minds. The word itself is something discrete. "Chair", "run", "love", "hate" – any one of these words are discrete symbols. But each of them relates to a huge complex of thoughts, of referents, relating to all of our life experiences. Even a seemingly simple noun has complex referents. For example, the word "chair" is connected with a host of things in our minds, different for each and every one of us. It's connected with things that I may call a chair, but nobody else would. We see that in art and poetry all the time.

The first people to talk philosophically about language were Greeks. One of the major functions of Plato's dialogues was to try to understand words, to figure out what something means. Plato created a whole system of thought just to try to explain how we get to the root concept of "chair". Those of you who have studied philosophy will remember his theory of ideals (or archetypes) – that there's an "ideal chair" out there, and the word "chair" represents the ideal chair. I don't want to go into that here, except to point out that even such a simple word was quite clearly understood by the Greeks to be very complicated. What we understand now is how intricately woven is the set of relationships between any given word symbol and all the myriad referents that it represents.

An additional complication is the nature of the interlinking of words with each other. Just as a word is linked with a whole web of experiences and thoughts, so too words are linked with each other through these webs. You see that in word association exercises. You learn a tremendous amount that is subtle about a person's individual way of looking at the world, just by understanding his/her free association of words. That's another way of saying that every word is organically linked to every other word in our mind somehow, and that unearthing these linkages that are very private and special to each of us is a key to understanding who we are. That's how rich the concept of "word" is.

Let's turn to the usefulness of these word symbols. Why did evolution give us language? What's the tremendous evolutionary benefit we get from having a word symbol that's so complex? Actually, it gives us two really significant advantages. The first is that it enables us to organize our thoughts in a much more efficient way. When you're bathing in an ocean of thoughts and experiences, you're overwhelmed by everything. Think of a pre-verbal child, and the tremendous perplexity of reality for that child because, among other things, not only is the child inexperienced, but by not having words, by not having that wonderful handle on which to hang sets of complexities, it's so much harder for the child to make sense out of his environment. There's just too much to process. Infants are brilliant. The pace at which they learn is staggering. Nevertheless, one of the reasons it takes them so long to learn certain things despite being so brilliant is because they don't have this wonderful shorthand, the word symbol. The word symbol is an organizational act of genius for evolution. It enables us, by short handing a huge bundle of experiences and referents into a symbol, to relate very complex experiences and thoughts in ways that we can then process and make use of. That's what conversations with ourselves are about. When we talk to ourselves, when we think to ourselves with words as opposed to pure meditation, we're doing this processing, we're reshuffling our ideas. We're trying to reorganize our thinking. We do it by shuffling words around and by reorganizing and putting them in different places.

In this connection, Alan White showed me a wonderful quote by Oliver Wendell Holmes; "I rough out my thoughts in talk as an artist models in clay. Spoken language is so plastic. You can pat and coax and spread and shade and rub out and fill up and stick on so easily when you work that soft material. There's nothing like it for modeling. Out of it comes the shapes which you turn into marble or bronze in your immortal books if you happen to write such." Nothing can describe better the way in which words are used by us to create and mold our own ideas.

But there's a second much greater evolutionary advantage that words give us that transcends even the ability to organize our own thoughts. Words enable one person to link into the modor of another. Through words, we can not only better organize the world on our own, but we can tap into how everybody else organizes the world and thereby immensely enrich our ability to understand reality and to make sense out of life. Suddenly, instead of my having only one mind – my own – with which to cope with reality, I have a tool by which I can probe other people's minds. Words are a medium of exchange between minds. They enable you to trade information concerning modors and thereby to make your domain of understanding much more universal.

This phenomenon is, in my opinion, quite miraculous. How it works is almost incomprehensible. How do I tap into your modor by using a word that might mean something so different to me than it does to you? Indeed, how can we ever get the same word to mean the same thing to both of us? It's a staggering task. Again, think of the struggle a child has to go through to figure out what a word means. It's not so much that the child has trouble with forming sounds. The sound part is the relatively easy part. The hard part is to figure out how to *use* the sound. "Why is that adult using that particular medium of exchange? What is the reference that I'm tapping into? If I use it, what will I elicit from her? If I say this word, what will happen?" Figuring out how to bridge the chasm between people's modors is the task of verbal communication. It's lengthy, it's arduous, and when successfully done, it's a tremendous achievement.

In order to understand better the social use of language, I'd like to talk briefly about what I call "concentric circles of language". The first place a person learns to use words is in the family, and that's no accident because, in the family circle, a child is subjected to the constant environment of the same people, the same parents, siblings, etc. It's a case of total immersion. It's like learning a new language for adults. What's the best way to learn a foreign language? In class? Forget about it. Take somebody, put them in France, don't give them a dictionary, and don't give them any companion who knows English – they'll learn French, for sure. Especially kids who don't have the inhibitions that adults have. Ask yourself, how does a seven year old who has never spoken a word of French, and who is dropped into Paris, end up chattering in French a month later? It's no different a question than how it happens that a two-year-old learns to speak the language that his/her family is using – by immersion, by constant exposure over and over again. The child starts to figure out what his parents or his siblings mean by specific words and tries to relate their use of the words to the symbolization that he's beginning to develop himself. "Love" is a perfect example. What does he do with "love"? He hears his parents say, "I love you," and then they jab him and practically squeeze the life out of him. He's wondering what this means. Or they plant a big wet kiss on him. What is he going to make out of this? He hears all kinds of cooing associated with the word. He's got to put this together coherently. Eventually, he forms a complex of experiences around that word symbol "love", and he starts using it. He may start using it in ludicrous ways, and then, of course, the adults around him interact with him and modify his use of the word.

Slowly, over a period of years of interaction between a child and his/her family, there develops an inner circle of language where the people in the family have a huge overlap in the referents of many of the words they use. Everybody is familiar with the "private language" that families develop. Every family has developed certain unique vocabularies and meanings. They can glance at each other and say a particular word, and a whole bundle of referents come to the fore, and they laugh, or wink at each other, and everybody else is clueless as to what is going on in that inner language circle.

In addition, as time passes, every social circle that we're in develops its own private language. But since we have less frequent contact, less immersion, in social circles than we do in the family circle, the overlap of word meanings among individuals decreases, and communication becomes more difficult. The challenge to understand becomes harder. So when you're in a social circle of people – say, those you're working with – you develop a common vocabulary, but it's not as intimate, not as comprehensive as the vocabulary in your family. When you're with your friends in school, you share a common vocabulary, but much of it is different from the one at work. There's a whole group of other words and other meanings, and even the same words have different meanings, when you're talking to your friends in your club. As the circle broadens, the ability to communicate, the ability to link into other people's conceptual schemes, becomes weaker and weaker. It becomes more challenging to know what they're talking about.

When a President stands up in front of the nation and uses words in a speech – any President, this is not a political statement – think of the challenge! Think of the challenge any person faces, standing up there with the Presidential seal behind him, and using words that are supposed to affect the affairs of the nation. There's no way everybody is going to have the same understanding of what he means. Every word has a slightly – or vastly – different meaning to each of the millions of people who are out there listening, and every connection is different, every linkage. How much more so with international relations, where you not only have to bridge differences of meaning using the same language, but you have to bridge translations between languages in which the very mechanics of putting words together are different.

I've gone into this at length because this ability to use words is a two-edged sword. This fabulous advantage, words, that evolution has given us – this ability to tap into other people's minds, this quantum leap of ability to understand the world, because suddenly I am not restricted to the use of my brain alone – has a down side; namely, that it's so difficult for me to figure out what these word-symbols mean to any other person. *That's what conversation is about.* Conversation is about is about using words over and over again, in whatever concentric language circle we're in, in order to try to learn what *we* mean and what *the other person* means by their use of words to comprehend the world. That's why conversation is so important, so insistent. That's why you have to engage in it for so many hours. What do you say when a person laconically gives a one-sentence reply to a very deep question you've asked? You say, "What is he talking about? I don't understand. That person never speaks. That person never says what's on his mind. You can never understand what's behind his thinking. He's always just giving you a one-sentence answer." And, if you challenge them and you say, "How come you're not saying more," they say, "I've said everything I have to say. That's what I mean." What you want to do is draw them out with more words and more words and more words. It's that sculpting process. "I want to know what you mean by this. What does it really mean to you and how can I relate that to what it means to me?" That's the whole purpose of those three hour telephone conversations that we have, that our teenage children have, and that our little 8 and 9-year-old children have. They're constantly trying to figure out, "How can I see the world more broadly, with the help of other minds as well as mine?" There's no greater tool that evolution gives us for success in life. The person who has mastered conversation, the person who has mastered the ability to tap into other people's modors, is the person best equipped to go out into a quickly changing world and tap into what's going on at any given moment. And the person who hasn't mastered this has been deprived of the most effective way possible to learn.

The power of conversation has been well recognized over the ages. The Greek academies were places where people walked around and talked. The scholars in Aristotle's school for philosophy were called "peripatetics", from the Greek for "people who walk around". They walked around and talked, and as they walked and talked, they developed great concepts, many of which were recorded in their immortal books. And in the other great ancient Western civilization, Judaic culture, the Rabbinic academies were all oral. Hundreds and thousands of learned rabbis over a period of 2,000 years talked and talked about the intricacies of Judaism, of Jewish law, of theology, of ethics, etc.

Or consider physics, your basic "hard" science. The most famous physics institute of the 20th century was the Niels Bohr Institute in Denmark. Bohr is the man who created the quantum theory of the atom, which lies at the heart of modern physics. He collected around himself the greatest physicists of his time, and hung out with them. That's what they did, they hung out. I'm using that phrase because we hear it a lot in this school. In his Institute, they'd come for a season to hang out. They'd take walks in the woods, they'd sail on the ocean, they'd swim, and what they treasured more than anything was talking. They talked about physics, they talked about theories, they talked about God, they talked about philosophy. What they were doing, all these greater and lesser physicists, was trying to understand about each other: "How does he see the world? What is he thinking?"

The fact is, we all spend a lot of time talking. There isn't a single person I know who doesn't spend a major part of their day talking. It's not just 100% functional talk. In fact, it's 99% non-functional talk. If you're honest with yourselves and you go through a day and ask yourself, "Of all the things that I say during the day, how much is directly functional?" I wager with you that you'd find out that well over 90% of what you say does not lead to a direct, useful outcome. It's mostly about learning meaning, exchanging meanings, and trying to figure out what's going on in other people's minds.

That's the primary importance of conversation. That's why kids do it, and that's why kids who are allowed to be free in a Sudbury school do it all the time. Parents sometimes worry that their children don't seem to be talking enough about functional things. "Why aren't they talking about algebra? I wouldn't mind it if they talked about algebra. I wouldn't mind it if they just sat down and read a play of Shakespeare." *In the long view of things, the ability to do algebra doesn't hold a candle to the ability to figure out what's going on in the world as it's changing under our eyes, and to tap into what other people are thinking about it.* If you have that ability, and you ever need some algebra along the way, you'll be skilled enough to get it very quickly because the ability to learn by tapping into other people's minds is the key here, not the ability to store any particular subject matter.

There is an odd paradox that I want to mention as I close. One of the things that the outside world always stresses is the need for greater communication. This is a very modern thing. When I was young, in the '40's and '50's, people did not talk all the time about the need for communication skills. My father and mother never mentioned the word. But as we became more sophisticated, in the '60's especially, that began to change. People began to realize that communication is an important skill. Nowadays, everybody's stressing communication. Yet, it's a paradox that even as people stress how important it is, they shy away from it in school. In traditional schools it's absolutely forbidden. In traditional schools, the last thing you want is for kids to open their mouths all day. "You're talking. You're disturbing the class." I had a professor who wouldn't even answer a question in class. He walked into the room the second the bell rang, and started writing on the board and lecturing. If somebody raised their hand because they didn't know what was going on, he would just look at them and say, "You're not paying your money to hear yourselves talk. You're paying money to hear me talk. If you have a question, come and see me in my office hours."

Our culture knows how important communication is, but in our schools, the place where we're supposedly preparing people to take their place in the real, ever-changing, rapidly-developing world, communication is kept to a minimum. What we at Sudbury Valley have learned over the past thirty years is that free communication is one of the greatest strengths of the school. When you let people be free, they communicate. They talk all day. And now we understand why.

So next time you see kids hanging out, think about how much they're getting out of it. Think of the school place as a modern day Aristotelian academy, where people develop their minds through talking.

I'd like to end with a wonderful short quote from an article written by Bruce Thomas[3]: "So what are words worth? Obviously a great deal. But words are to our conscious social selves as air is to our physical selves – an aspect of life so taken for granted, so familiar in its essentiality that it becomes invisible. Moreover, in their form as conversation, words are a constituent of school that is deeply troublesome to both psychometricians and economists. How do you measure the relationship of conversation to student achievement? How do you measure conversation at all? How does the economist calculate an input that expands and contracts all the time, that can be created in an abundance that contradicts the scarcity-driven character of our traditional schools? Untidy and elusive, conversation lies beyond the range of measurement and defies incorporation as a variable into cause-and-effect relationships. But that's alright. Let's all just keep talking."

---

[3] "What Are Words Worth?", *Sudbury Valley School Journal* (Vol. 27, No. 2), p. 39.

What Is the Role of Parents?

Today I would like to focus on is what we have learned about the answer to the question, "What *is* the role of parents?" – a question that so many of us hear around the school in so many different contexts.

Let me go back and tell you what we were thinking when we first started the school. The question of parents and their role in the school is dealt with in the By-laws of the school Corporation, so it is obviously something that had been given thought, albeit in the rather narrow context of the legal role of parents in the school corporate structure. At least for me, one of the reasons parents were given a voice was my reaction to reading A. S. Neill's book, *Summerhill*. Back in the sixties, when the book first appeared, it hit the American scene with a very loud roar. It influenced an awful lot of people and certainly had a tremendous effect on us. One of the things that Neill comes back to over and over again is his dislike for parents. For him, parents are "the enemy", a position he came to from a therapeutic point of view. He was a staunch Reichean, and a devoted student of psychoanalysis, and he firmly believed that parents are the source of most of the world's troubles. In line with this view, he set up his school in a way that was openly antagonistic to parents. He didn't want parents to have anything to do with Summerhill. Not only didn't they have a say, which is the last thing on earth that would have entered his mind, but he didn't want them around in any way, shape, or form. If you wanted to enroll your child in the school, and you wrote and asked to visit the school, the usual answer would be, "Send your kid, but stay at home yourself."

We felt, just instinctively back then, without thinking it through in depth, that this is not the kind of situation we wanted. Part of the reason was that most of the founders were parents. Whatever our role was going to be in the school directly, one thing we were sure of was that we wanted to be involved in setting up a school in which we could somehow stay involved, in which we weren't "the enemy". That's what led to the concept of the Assembly in the very first set of By-laws, a concept which has retained its original significance to this day. The Assembly was to be the policy-making body of the school, and it was to include everybody who had a stake in the school – staff members, Trustees, public members, and also, in addition, *parents*. That was a big thing. That meant that parents had not just "input", but an actual vote, equal to that of everyone else. For us, that was a big step.

That still didn't give us much of a concept of what the role of parents is in the school. The vote is just a small piece of the role. We struggled with that over the first few years, but the topic wasn't front and center. Not that many people cared. Then, about fifteen years ago, we started to encounter a problem. There were some parents who, for one reason or another, started hanging out at school. That made a number of students uncomfortable. There was nothing malicious about the situation. On any given day, you might find a parent in the sewing room, innocently sitting and reading, and everybody in the sewing room felt funny because there was a parent sitting there. This person wasn't doing anything bad, wasn't intervening, wasn't criticizing. She just existed in that space, and that was enough to make people uncomfortable.

So it became clear that kids didn't want parents just hanging out at school. They didn't want *any* adults, not just parents, being at school on a regular basis unless they had been invited to do so by the School Meeting. That made us start thinking about the whole question of parents in the community. We had given parents a central role in the Assembly. We had made it clear, from the beginning, that it was ok for parents to drop in when they brought their kids – to walk down, and chat a bit with kids, staff, or each other, before they leave. What else was wanted by, or from, parents in the school community? We realized we had to give that a lot more thought.

The more we contemplated the question, the clearer it became that the real issue, first and foremost, was that of parents' role *in life*, rather than simply their role in school. We came to see that in order for us to understand what parents should be doing in school, we had to have a much clearer picture of what parents should be doing as parents in the family. If we don't understand their role in life, we're not really going to understand their role in school.[4]

As you think about it, you realize very early in the game that a parent's role is problematic, even paradoxical. That's because, biologically, parents are

---

[4] This is an example of a principle to which I was introduced by a good friend in graduate school, many years ago. He used to say, "If you have a problem that you can't solve, one that is really intractable, turn to a larger problem which has your problem as a subset. Often you'll find that the solution to the larger problem is easier than the solution to the one you focused on in the beginning, and then the original problem will solve itself."

Nature's agents for nurturing the transition of a child from dependence to independence. Basically, the end goal is the independence of the child. The species wouldn't survive if each new generation didn't manage to become independent of the old one. You are born, you have a mother and father, but basically your end goal is to leave them.

Now, the problem and the paradox come in because the means of getting to this goal involves an initial stage of dependence. That's inevitable, because the child, at birth, is completely dependent, and for many years continues to have a considerable degree of dependence. From the beginning, you have a difficult and paradoxical situation – a situation where we're here as parents, to nurture our dependent children towards independence. The end goal is independence; the means involves dependence. These are two contradictory concepts which have to coexist in the parent-child relationship from the beginning, which tells you right from the outset that you're in trouble, that the concept of parenting does not have clear answers to questions, because any concept rooted in an inherently contradictory paradox is going to lead to contradictory, conflicting, and difficult, judgmental, answers.

I cannot sufficiently stress how crucial this initial dependency is to the relationship. It leaves an indelible mark on the relationship between child and parent. In the early days of a child's life, his/her very survival depends on learning to read all the subtle signs of approval and disapproval of the parent. It's as simple as that. Children have to figure out, practically from the moment of birth, how they're going to get their needs met from their parent in this dependency relationship. Of course, I'm not talking about figuring it out cognitively, with words and with logical formulations. I'm talking about figuring it out in a real life situation, *feeling* it. There's nobody in the world who's more hypersensitive to someone else's emotions than a child is to the parent. Our children read us like no one else – better than our spouses, better than our best friends. They read us in ways that we can't even begin to comprehend, and they respond emotionally, at the deepest survival levels, to every little nuance of our emotions, not only those exhibited towards them, but also those exhibited towards other people. Children simply couldn't make it if they didn't have this innate skill.

The fact is that neither a parent nor a child can erase or forget that early dependent phase. It stays with us through life, with the parents and with the children. It colors the relationship forever, even as adults. Our parents' wishes and views always have a different weight with us, pro or con, than those of any other adult. I know how I felt in the presence of my father, who died at the age of 91. Here I was, in my late 50's, and I was still his "kid". There's no way I could be anything different. It doesn't make any difference if we have families, if we have successful lives – when we're in the presence of our parents, no matter how much we have declared our independence of them, no matter whether we're close to them or distant from them, love them or hate them, that hypersensitivity to the way they react is still there.

There's an additional problem: even though the end goal of this relationship is independence for the child, on both sides of this relationship there is a residual yearning for maintaining the state of dependency. The parent yearns for that dependency to go on just a little because an independent child means a sense of loss, a departure, grief. I'm not talking about an active desire to keep a child dependent, but rather about something that comes from within. "I want them to be independent, but I know that when they're gone I'm going to miss them." Just a slight yearning for dependency, which throws a monkeywrench into how we behave to our children. In the child, there's that residual yearning too, because it's nice to be taken care of: "Sure, I want to be independent. I want to go out into the world. I want to earn a living. I want to have my own apartment. I want my own car." They're all quick to say this, but they still don't mind when you do the laundry or when you give them a good meal or you take care of little things for them. It's nice to be taken care of. It's that little residual yearning for dependency left in all of us as we grow up.

Actually, this can be dangerous, because that yearning for dependency, if it isn't fulfilled with a parent, can get transferred in not very healthy ways to a company or a sect or a community or some other situation where you never let go of that feeling and you become a dependent adult.

To summarize, the development of independence in a child has to contend not only with the inherent problems of dependency, but also with both the parents' and children's reluctance to let go of the dependence. Despite all this, our role as parents is to somewhat smooth our children's path to independence. Unfortunately, this means that there are occasions when we're going to have to intervene. Intervention is necessary because *smoothing the path* is an active, not a passive, endeavor. Helping a child become independent isn't just setting him/her down and saying, "You're independent." It's doing a whole series of active things that will make it possible for a child to grow up according to his/her inner direction. Thus, even as we prepare the child for independence, we're constantly intervening in the child's life, which is part and parcel of the contradiction that I have been talking about.

There are, broadly speaking, two kinds of intervention. First, there are interventions in big decisions. These are absolutely inescapable; they are the decisions in life that are responsible for the survival of the family as a whole. For example, "Where are we going to live? How am I going to earn a living?" These are decisions that are made with a view toward the overall survival needs of the family, and they obviously impact children in a major way. If I grow up in one town and then find out that, in order to continue to feed my children, I have to move to another town, that means uprooting the children from their friends, from their context, from the home in which they have been comfortable, etc. These are wrenching outcomes for a child. As adults, we know why we're making them, and it might be hard for us, too, to leave our friends and our community, etc.; but we know why we're doing it. For the children, no matter how much you explain to them, no matter how old they are, this is a wrenching intervention that deeply affects their lives and that they really don't feel they need. "Making a living" is something you can't explain to children on an emotional level, because children aren't responsible for feeding themselves. They take it for granted that their parents are going to feed them. "Why do we have to move? I understand that we have to eat – you're *supposed to* feed me. But why do we have to *move?*" It doesn't connect emotionally.

Big interventions involve the decisions that we *have to* make. We hope that the children will somehow survive them; most of the time they somehow do. We really can't help too much by explaining. Basically, it's a case of, "This is the way it is. This is where we've got to live. I'm sorry it hurts you. I'm sure you'll make new friends. I'm sure you'll meet new people."

But the road to independence is made easier if the intervention in *smaller* decisions is minimized. That is where we all struggle the most: first of all, distinguishing between big decisions and lesser decisions that we can let go of; and secondly, letting go even when we've found out. It's hard to exaggerate how difficult that is. For instance, clothes. This is a classic example. The reality is that what clothes our children wear is not a major intervention that we have to make in order to smooth their path to independence. As long as they physically have enough on at any given time to feel comfortable, so that *they* don't feel cold and *they* don't feel uncomfortable, we have to face the fact that it's ok. This is the reality. None of us, I dare say, can live up to that reality fully. We always think we can judge better than our children when they're cold. Sometimes, when dealing with such a lesser decision, we convert it, in our minds – because we're struggling with it – into a major decision, in order to justify our intervention. We say, "They'll catch cold. They'll get pneumonia. They'll be sick." We turn it into a matter of survival. Whereas all the evidence available is that children who are allowed to go with their own instincts in matters relating to clothing don't get any sicker than children who aren't. But the evidence has nothing to do with what we feel.

Food is another example. Food is such a bugaboo. We are so sure our kids will not survive if we don't make them eat the "right" foods. We had somebody in the school, thirty years ago, who ate practically nothing but Poptarts. Day after day, year after year. It's impossible to understand biologically what happened here, but the kid grew. The funniest part about all this was that, while our kids were getting sick right and left with flus and colds and stuff like that through the winter, this kid was never sick. I don't know what that proves. Probably, for the most part, except in the most extreme cases of clear-cut eating disorders, which I certainly don't minimize, what food a kid eats, or when s/he eats it, is a lesser intervention. Whether we all have a family dinner together is a parental decision, not necessarily a survival one, not necessarily one that interests kids at every age. Is it a big enough decision to warrant intervention as we smooth our children's path to independence? Or is it a lesser one that we can let go of and say, "This is part of their becoming independent. Let them be."

The list goes on and on. These are the questions we grapple with, but as we grapple with them, if we're being fair to our role as parents, we have to ask ourselves constantly, "Is this something where intervention is really essential?" – because every intervention is a step away from independence. Each of us will answer differently. I'm the last person to judge your answers any more than I want mine judged. But what should be the same for all of us, is that we *ask that question*. It's when we stop asking that question that we start doing damage to that role that we were assigned as parents – easing the way for the child's transition to independence.

The fact of intervention differentiates a parental role from that of all others in a functional way. No one else in our society has the right to intervene. As parents, we have this right. Otherwise, in our very individualistic culture, we've developed the long-standing position that we don't intervene in each other's child-rearing practices. If I see a parent doing something that is, in my judgment, clearly a bad child-rearing practice, I have to keep it to myself. I may share it with my wife; we may shake our heads about it at home, in the privacy of our bedroom. But if I criticize the parent directly, I'm out of line. I've overstepped societal bounds.

Another deep difference between parents and all others is the question of unconditional love. You don't get it anywhere else except in the family. An adult can smooth talk any child and can even, maybe, mean it. "I love you. I feel like you're my child. I feel as warmly to you as if you were a member of my family." Many of us have actually said this to children, meaning it. But no kid is fooled. Every kid knows that, when you say that, you mean it up to a point, and they all generally know exactly what that point is.

We are almost ready to give an answer to the narrower question: What is the role of parents in the school? We have to answer one more question first: What is the *school's* role? Interestingly, we find a similarity to the parents' role. The school's role in society, in general, is to create an environment where children can prepare themselves for adulthood. In other words, the school is a community institution established to help prepare a child to be an independent member of the community. This means that a school has to be a place where children can develop whatever skills they need to adapt to adult society – cognitive and technical skills to become economically independent, and social skills to participate in adult society.

At Sudbury Valley, we concluded that our way of doing this is to give children practical, hands-on experience in being independent right from the beginning. Not some set of skills that might (or might not) help them to become independent later, but practical, hands-on skills in being independent now, with the idea that they'll become better at them as they grow older, because that's what they want to do. We also give them an opportunity to enjoy practical, hands-on experience in forming real world relationships. We let them figure out and experience, from the youngest age, how you deal with other kids and with adults. We don't guide them, or group them, or give the various assists that other schools give them. We say, "You've got to do this on your own, through hands-on experience."

This is a mission that we take very seriously. It can be very hard for parents. Parents represent unconditional love. It's painful for parents when children come home and talk about all the frustrations that they've had during the day: "This one was mean to me. That one wouldn't play with me. I have no friends." For the school, this is part and parcel of the reality of the world. Adults have to work hard to make friends. Adults have to learn how to live with the fact that there are enemies out there who wish us evil. Adults have to figure out who their friends are and who their ill-wishers are, and how to get along with both. Sudbury Valley has always said, "Give children practical, hands-on experience with this hard work from day one. It's the best, quickest, easiest and longest-lasting way to learn."

We also believe that preparing kids for independence in society means giving kids hands-on experience with democracy, with existing in a place where decisions are made by the community. Adults have to live with decisions that they don't like, every day, and they have to realize that part of the beauty of living in a democratic community is swallowing your disappointment when you don't get your way.

Now we are in a position to understand why, generally speaking, parents don't belong as a regular daily feature of the school. It's not because parents are evil. On the contrary. It's because parents, as parents, have inherent tasks in child rearing that are different from the inherent tasks that our school has set itself up to do. The parental role tends to be in conflict with the role of a school that's devoted primarily to giving hands-on experience to individual independence, to democratic decision making, and to working your own way toward social relationships.

What does this imply about staff parents in the school? The problem of staff parents has been a devilish one from day one. I've been one, many of the founders were, and we have several people on the staff today who are parents. Every one of them will tell you the same thing: being a staff parent is no easy ride for the parent, and it's often no fun for the children. If there had been a second Sudbury school in another town within any kind of commuting distance, we'd have gladly sent our kids there. It takes a tremendous amount of restraint and discipline to coexist in our school, and there are always problems.

I'll give you a simple example that any parent can relate to. It takes restraint in JC matters. One year, our oldest child had a record of being brought up more than anybody else. He was disturbingly noisy by nature. He defined the term "disturbingly noisy", and he was brought up all the time. As parents, we had to be absolutely clear in our heads that the judicial process had to take its course, and that we could have nothing to do with it. We couldn't talk to anybody on the Judicial Committee, and we couldn't intervene in any way. Our attitude toward our child at school had to be: "You made your bed, you sleep in it. The JC has to deal with it. That's their business." For loving parents, that takes a lot of self-discipline. For some people on the staff, it was never that easy to do. For others, it was easier. But it was always a challenge.

From the child's point of view, it's no fun either. They can keep out of our sight. That part isn't that hard. Even though it's a tiny school, it's amazing how easy it is for people to stay out of the sight of somebody they don't want to be around. I can honestly say that in all the years our three kids were at the school, I didn't see them very much during the day. I imagine that they maneuvered that more than I did. I didn't consciously avoid them, but I'll bet they consciously avoided me, which would make sense. They couldn't avoid the fact that their dad was a staff member. They couldn't avoid hearing the inevitable unpleasant things that are said about anybody at school, kid or adult, but certainly about staff members at certain times, especially when "that bastard brought me up for the fifth time" and "that bastard" happens to be your father! It's hard.

    Yet, it seems to be a fact that you really can't get a school started and, probably, you can't keep a school going indefinitely, unless there are a certain number of people on the staff who are so absolutely committed to it, because their children are there, that they'll walk through hellfire in order to keep it going. So, it's an uncomfortable situation, but it's apparently necessary, at this stage of development of Sudbury schools, to have on the staff at least some people as committed to the survival of the school as parents tend to be. The protection the school community has is that the staff is elected, without tenure, every single year, and more than one parent/staff member has been dropped from the school's staff in the course of the years while their children were still in school. So you can see how difficult a problem that is all around.

Let me digress briefly in order to elucidate my point with another example. You hear a lot these days about homeschooling. There is a sub-group of homeschoolers who call themselves "unschoolers", many of whom claim to be educating their children in a manner virtually identical to ours at Sudbury Valley. These are people who say honestly, and mean honestly, "We believe in giving our children the freedom to do whatever they want, and not intervening in their activities. If they want to play all day, they can play all day. Whatever they want to do is fine with us. We're just there to be supportive of their wishes." Often, they write to us and say, "We're just like Sudbury Valley."

It is, however, the complexity of the parental role that is at the heart of the difference between us and any form of unschooling. People talk about all sorts of problems with unschooling, and there are heated debates about it. For example, there's a question of whether unschooling can provide a good socialization mechanism for kids, when the kids spend most of their time at home. To be sure, there are situations where parents of unschoolers get together a few times a week at each others' houses to provide socialization. Then there's the matter of the absence of a democratic environment. There's no way an unschooling situation can provide a hands-on democratic environment, because the parents are there all the time and they are making, daily, all the key decisions that have to be made.

Then there's the problem of the parental tendency, however much they deny it, to shelter their children. In unschooling situations, there's a lack of exposure to real world constraints. One of the beautiful things about watching kids grow at Sudbury Valley, from age four and up, is seeing them learn how to use the system to get their needs, how to understand the politics and the relationships in the school. It is impressive and amazing to watch a five or ten year old figure out, "I want the school to get X; how do I do it?" They'll go to somebody and ask about the School Meeting. "What do I do? How do I write a motion? Will you help me?" There are very few things that are more moving than to sit in a School Meeting and see three or four seven year olds sitting through a two hour meeting, quiet as mice, until their item comes up for discussion. They can be the most active kids in the school, but they'll be sitting there quietly, waiting for their agenda item to come up. They know that they have to raise their hands and to explain what they want, and answer questions. That kind of learning – how to overcome real world constraints, which is part and parcel of being adults –

you can't get in an unschooling environment, because you're negotiating with your parents, not with a larger, more impersonal community.

I think, however, that the key element that differentiates us from an unschooling environment, which is why I brought it up, is the inherent problem of hypersensitivity that I talked about. The fact is that when you're in your parents' presence, you cannot help being hypersensitive to their reactions. There are so many subtle ways that parents have of indicating what it is that would really please them, even as they're saying – and believing – that they don't care what you do. "All I want is for you to be happy and do what you want." "Well, this is what I want. I want to buy a drum set," at age seven. There's just that moment of parental hesitancy, maybe, that glimmer of disapproval – and the illusion of free choice is shattered. Parental control is not something that you can relinquish. You can't will it away. You can't voluntarily give it up.

Let me summarize what we've learned about the role of parents in the school. The role of parents in the school is based on their role in life. First of all, parents are involved in the big decisions that have to do with the school, just like they are in life. It's part of the inevitable role of parents that we talked about earlier. For example, they make the big decision of sending the child to this school in the first place. No matter how much we say that it's up to the child – and usually, to a certain extent, it *is* up to the child – the reality is that it's a parental decision to send the child to the school. The parents have to find a way to raise the money. The parents have to be the ones to show that they're really behind this decision and want it to happen. For this decision to have any meaning, parents have to give real support to the school and to the idea of the child being at the school, because there's no point in making the decision to send the kid to the school and not being behind it. We're behind every other big decision we make for our kids; why wouldn't we be behind this one? That's something that is so essential for parents to understand in this school. And it's so hard to do, because sending a child to this school differs from other big decisions that we make, *because the big decision to send the kid to this school also involves, in each of the parents, a big decision to allow the child to undergo something that we didn't undergo as children, and that's alien to our experience.* That's what makes this such a difficult big decision.

If we want to be true to our role as parents, we have to be 100% supportive of that big decision. We made it; now we have to stand behind it. If we make it and don't stand behind it, don't be surprised later if the kids are confused, don't know where we stand, and don't benefit from the school. That kind of parental equivocation they pick up in a minute. And being behind the decision means, in particular, that we have to be behind the choices our children make here. I can't stress that enough. Making the decision to send the kid to this school involves supporting their decisions while they're here. If we can't do that, we shouldn't send them here. That is hard, because it means not raising that eyebrow that we might have raised when we hear that they played all day or talked all day or didn't put their shoes on in the snow or whatever. No raised eyebrows. No, "That sounds very nice," with a little touch of tension in the voice. It's hard, but it's the way we've got to be if we're going to stand by that big decision.

The other way that the parents are involved in the big decisions is through the Assembly. In this context, the Assembly makes sense. It makes sense for the parents, a few times a year, to be involved in the big questions. Parents help decide the budget, and the tuition, and many other large questions that have to do with the culture of the school and how it develops. So parental participation in the Assembly really makes sense within a broader context.

That, then, is what I've learned during the past thirty years. I guess in 1968 we were lucky to have figured out the right place to position the parents in the school. The Assembly worked out to make sense – the idea that the parents are involved in the large decisions, but not in the myriad day-to-day decisions. They're members of the Assembly, not of the School Meeting. They have input into the large decisions of the school, but they don't look over their children's shoulders – a perfect match between a school that provides children with hands-on experience for independence, and parenting, whose role it is to smooth the path towards independence.

The Significance of the Democratic Model:
Self-Esteem, Self-Rule, and Self-Motivation

It may sound like a strange thing to talk about the significance of the democratic model in a school like ours, because the democratic model is so embedded in the school, and has been from day one. In fact, though, our understanding of what the model means has undergone significant development during the past thirty years.

The very first pamphlet that came out announcing the school didn't mention democracy[5]. It was titled "A Radical Proposal", and it was written in 1965. It said, "The guiding principle of the school is that every

---

[5] These early documents are all collected in the book *Announcing a New School* (Sudbury Valley School Press; Framingham, 1973), which is the history of the beginnings of the school, with appendices that contain photocopies of many of these documents. They're quaint now, when you look at them, over 30 years later.

member be free to pursue his own interests entirely wherever they may lead." Of course, that's still a guiding principle of the school, but that doesn't relate, at least in an obvious way, to democracy. Our first public flyer barely mentions democracy, except for the statement, "All people connected with school share responsibility for the school's operation." There you see something explicit, but not the "d" word. The first official brochure of the school, which was called *About the Sudbury Valley School*, was written in 1968. Among other things it lists nine key features of the school, and democracy appears there as number 8: "All members of the school community participate in regulating the school's activities." That's it. That's the basic statement – simple and straightforward. The brochure goes on to say that we feel that all nine listed features are organically related, but not much is said about *how* democracy is organically related to all the other features. It was a good statement, but not too much meat on it; and that, I believe, reflects the state of our thinking at the time. We knew we had a good thing, and I guess we didn't feel, at the time, that it was necessary to elaborate more.

Democracy was built into the Corporate Bylaws from the beginning: we had the School Meeting, which consisted of all students and staff and regulated the school's daily affairs; and we had the Assembly, which included students, staff, and parents, and made all the general policy decisions of the school.

Why did we embed democracy in the school's structure? What was it doing there in the early years? What was its function?

We had an answer back then, one that had to do with school as a training ground for a democratic society. Sudbury Valley has always been a hands-on place. It's a place where children learn not just – or primarily – by talking about things, but rather through experience. For example, we don't talk about ethics. Moral decisions are a part of everyday life in this school. Our attitude towards that is similar to our attitude toward everything: the way you gain knowledge and wisdom in any area is by experiencing activity in that area.

For us, the idea of democracy in the school was a a socio-political goal: training for future citizenship. After all, what are schools for? They are a place where children prepare to be adults in society. One characteristic of society in the United States is that it is a democracy. Our stance in school was that if you want to train good citizens to live in a democracy, the way to do it is to give them hands-on experience in democracy – not to talk about it, not to preach about it, but to make them comfortable with it from day one.

I'd like to show you how consistent that aspect of our understanding of democracy has been through the years. In the first full-length book that we published, *The Crisis in American Education*[6], which was a really good seller in the early '70's and is still in print, we wrote: "There are three root ideas underlying the ethical, political and social structure of the United States. These three ideas serve as guiding principles for the nation as a whole. The first is the idea of individual rights. Every person is endowed with certain inalienable rights that belong to him as his own. The second root idea is political democracy. All decisions governing the community are decided by the community in a politically democratic way. The third right is equal opportunity. Every person has an equal chance to obtain any goal."

We go on to say: "One would think that our schools would be the most persistent and vigorous expounders of these root ideas. After all, what is the ultimate goal of education if not to prepare the nation's youth for a lifetime of responsible, mature citizenship?" For us, preparing for adulthood in a democratic society implied hands-on experience with living in a democratic milieu.

---

[6] (Sudbury Valley School Press; Framingham, 1970)

That was written in 1970. Here, now, is what I said in a presentation entitled, "Education for Democracy Demands Democratic Schools" that I made to the first international conference on democratic education, in 1993[7]: "As believers in democracy, we take upon ourselves the ... responsibility of seeing to its continuation. How then are we to educate for democracy in those schools where we set out to do so? ... To educate successfully for democracy, the real life surroundings of the children we seek to educate must be democratic in every respect, through and through, to the core and down to the last detail. The world of the children we want to reach must be a democratic reality, so the children wishing to master it will have no choice but to master the whole intricacy of its democratic structure. Education for democracy demands democratic schools. There is no other way to make it effective."

---

[7] The conference was held in Jerusalem, and people attended from all over the world. Invited were many academicians, but almost no representatives of schools that claim to practice democracy in one form or another. In fact, ours was the only school invited to make a presentation, thanks to the efforts of Yakov Hecht, who was director of the Democratic School of Hadera, Israel, and who was not himself asked to make a presentation!

The Significance of the Democratic Model

So you can see that the theme of school democracy as an essential component of the social part of education has been a constant throughout the years.

We didn't focus, however, on the relationship between democracy and other values of the school, even though we talked about its interrelatedness to other values. We didn't really grasp it. Last year, a lot of the pieces fell into place for me personally. It happened as one of those "eureka" experiences which really don't mean that much to somebody else who doesn't have it. The setting was an informal Assembly discussion group meeting. Sitting around in a room were a group of parents and some students and staff members. One of the parents asked the students in the room, "What is the most important element of the school for you?" The questioner didn't want to know what the staff felt was most important; she wanted to know what the *students* thought was most important. Without hesitating, Ben Day replied, "Democracy," and he talked briefly about empowerment. That was what democracy meant to him. The last thing I expected a student to say in response to that question was "democracy". I expected "freedom", "the ability to do what you want" – but not democracy.

I began to think hard about this. He was talking about democracy as empowerment; he wasn't talking about School Meetings as a socio-political process, as a method for deciding legislative agendas and governing communities. He was talking about something a little different, closely related to it. That's when I started focusing on the larger question: what is the significance of democracy *in society*? Understanding its significance in American culture must precede our ability to grasp its significance in the school.

In the American version of democracy, the idea of personal empowerment is at the heart of everything. You see it in the Declaration of Independence and in the Bill of Rights – in the idea that all men are created equal, and are endowed by their creator with certain inalienable rights, among which are life, liberty and the pursuit of happiness. In America, the individual is supreme vis-a-vis the community. The community exists for the purpose of furthering individual happiness.

What an incredible concept! It's completely different from the classical idea of democracy in ancient Greece, which was a purely political process. That had to do with how you decide issues in a society. You don't have a king make the decision, or a bunch of noblemen, or a small oligarchy; you have *everybody* get together and vote, and the side with the most votes wins., It's not surprising that most serious philosophers in ancient Greece came to the conclusion that democracy is a terrible form of government. They saw it as simply a question of who sways the most votes at any particular time, and they could think of no reason why that is any better than a king. Somebody like Plato would argue at great length and very successfully that in fact it's worse than a king, because a king can be taught to think philosophically about deep issues, whereas you can't expect much from the average bunch of people who get together in a big coliseum and vote. Likely as not, they'll just be swayed by the latest fad. There's no mention of the individual in the Greek concept of democracy. The individual is not what's important. What's important is the city-state.

Even England, today, does not have a written Constitution or a Bill of Rights. We come from English roots, yet the English don't have a Bill of Rights. For example, England has censorship of the press in certain areas, where the government can tell the newspapers, "You don't print this." England still has a class society. It still has a House of Lords. The idea of trial by a jury of peers, for example, means, among other things, that if you're a Lord, if you commit a murder, your jury is the House of Lords. You don't go to court with a regular jury like all the rest of the people. You go to the House of Lords. Very different from the U.S.A.

In America, the whole idea of democracy is that it's a social order designed to protect and promote aspects of individual fulfillment. I'd like to name three aspects of individual fulfillment that are specifically promoted. One is the idea of individual self rule, of empowerment. You're the master of your fate. You're the person who decides what you do with your life. True, sometimes you can get that taken away from you. If you commit a crime and end up in jail, you're no longer quite the master of your life. But, generally speaking, citizens control their own fate. One of the interesting aspects of self rule in this country is the incredible mobility of its citizens. Throughout most of history and most of the world, people weren't free to travel. I don't mean for tourist purposes. I mean to go somewhere else to change their destiny, to change the way they live. Even now, we're really the only heavily populated continental country in which individual human beings can decide where they want to live and nobody can say a word about it. You don't have to have individual ID's or passports. You don't have to show the person in the railroad station a travel permit in order to get a train ticket to go from Boston to Washington. There are no borders to cross, no barriers to overcome.

A second aspect of individual fulfillment is self motivation. In America, we protect the ability of individuals to start their own projects and to carry them out. That's the heart of the entrepreneurial spirit of this country. It's nothing for people here to say, "I want to start something new. I want to start a business. I want to write poems. I want to market some new idea." People do it all the time and, in the post-industrial age, it's becoming more the norm than the exception. We take it for granted. It's embedded in our culture.

You can't do this in most of the world today, even in many Western democracies. Because most of the world starts with the idea that the government exists primarily for the benefit of society as a whole. Its first objective is to regulate the individual through a host of rules that everybody has to obey for the greater good of the community. That's why people all over the world complain that it's so hard to be creative and entrepreneurial. In this country, too, we grouse about how much the government controls us. But the fact is that there's no place in the world where the government is less on people's backs, because the starting point here is what each individual person wants for his/her own future.

The third aspect of empowerment is the concept of self esteem, by which I mean the feeling that I am as worthy as my neighbor. It's a fact of American history that we have never had a formal class structure in our society. From the beginning, ours was a society where we didn't accord differential privilege based on education, heredity, money, or any other criterion. That doesn't mean that there aren't informal situations where people look down their noses at each other, but those run counter to the culture, which holds as a basic tenet that no matter where you were born, or who you are, you're as good as the next person.

All these aspects of personal empowerment were applied at first, in this country, to white adult males who were land owners. As time passed, they were extended to white adult males who didn't own land, then to adult males of all races, and finally to adults of both genders. The essence was there from the outset. The application spread slowly as the decades went by. It hasn't quite reached children yet. That's one of the key features of Sudbury Valley, as we shall see.

I would like to digress briefly to discuss something that I have found to be significant. One of the things I kept wondering about is the question: where did this uniquely American concept of democracy come from? What is its origin? Democracy has been practiced one way or another from ancient times, and yet the American take on it is notably different and original. How did this happen? The answer, I think, is rooted in geo-politics, and I think that understanding it helps us appreciate it better. Basically, it has to do with the history of how North America was settled, in the context of European colonization across the globe.

Let's take ourselves back to the 15th century. This is the beginning of the so-called "modern era" from the

Europeans' point of view, the period when European civilization became the dominant technological civilization in the world. For a variety of reasons, Europe emerged as a powerful force that overwhelmed the ability of the rest of the world to withstand its encroachment. That was, historically, a new phenomenon. Europe became a continent bursting with strength, and with the desire to conquer or dominate the rest of the world, militarily and economically. In particular, Europeans were seized with the desire to expand their influence and trade to the Far East, to those exotic lands that have spices and silks and other wonderful things that you can bring back home and sell at a tremendous profit. In short, if you study the history of that period, you find that Europe is focused on the wealth of the Far East.

Now, if you're in Europe and you want to get to the Far East, how do you do it? Suppose you want to go through the Mediterranean and the Middle East. It turns out that the Italian city-states have a stranglehold on the Mediterranean trade, that has made the Italians the richest people in Europe for a couple of hundred years. Everybody else is looking with envy at Italy. Who else is a maritime power in that period? Only a few countries: Holland, Spain, Portugal, England, and France. First in line is Portugal. They have kings who are real seafarers and they decide, "We're going to get the Eastern trade too. We can't go through the Mediterranean because the Italians have it locked up. We're going to see if we can go the other way around." So they start working their way around Africa, and finally get around the Cape of Good Hope and up the other side until they reach India and tie up that route. That's what's going on in the Columbus story. After all, why should anyone care about an Italian seafarer coming to Spanish court and talking about sailing to the Far East? Because the Spanish court is dying to participate in the Eastern trade, and all known routes are locked up! Along comes this guy and says, "Go this way. It's open." So they give it a try.

This is where the story becomes interesting. They go West and they hit the Caribbean, Central America, and South America. Of course they don't find the Far East; they find something a hundred times better! They find ancient civilizations that are fantastically wealthy. So, almost overnight, the Spaniards take over that whole region, milk its wealth, and bring it home. Spain becomes the richest country in Europe for some 150 years. It's hard for us to imagine, given the current condition of Spain. Today, you certainly wouldn't think of Spain as one of the greatest powers on earth for almost two centuries at the dawn of the modern era.

In North America, by contrast, there wasn't any wealth to speak of. *This is the key to the uniqueness of the*

North American experience. There are no Incan or Mayan civilizations in North America. North America is a continent in which there are hundreds of different native cultures, none of which possess fabulous wealth. The Spaniards roamed all over North America trying to find gold and silver, and they couldn't find any at hand. So they left it alone – a whole continent, with an inhospitable climate, and no wealth. It's all that's left for the English and French! The French do what the Norsemen before them did in North America in the 10th century, and what the Russians did in Siberia: they trade in furs. They travel through all the major river systems of North America – the St. Lawrence, the Mississippi, the Missouri – and end up claiming all central North America for the French king. Which leaves England.

Now, what does England do? Bad climate means nothing to them. This is like home: rain, snow, cold, misery. The English have a different problem. Over time, they have developed more personal and political freedom than any other country in Europe. In England, some of the bonds of autocracy have been loosened. There is a form of representative government. Remember, we're talking about the fifteenth and sixteenth century. English kings are still supreme. Common people are only marginally empowered. But there's a lot more freedom there than anywhere else, and the thing about freedom is that, once you get a little bit of it, it whets the appetite. In England, you have an awful lot of dissidents, because that's what freedom breeds. European continental powers knew what to do with dissidents. They killed them. They put them in jail. They shut them up. The English did some of that too, but not quite as much. So they ended up with a country in which people with different views of how life ought to be are stirring things up and making trouble.

This is the ideal setting for a whole new concept within the framework of colonialism: *colonization*. Not going over to rule and exploit a local population, which is what the Spaniards did, and what the English did when they plundered India a few centuries later, but going to a new continent and *settling there* because you want to live your life the way you want to live it and not be bugged by the ruling authorities.

We all studied this in social studies. The Quakers, for example. They're not happy in England. They don't like the established church. They see an opportunity to depart to a place that no one wants but the English. They come to the king and say, "Give us a piece of this new land." The king is delighted. He can get rid of these malcontents. He can ship them over to America! And who goes? What kind of person picks himself up in the 1600's and 1700's, leaves his home, leaves his native country, leaves his friends, leaves his support group, leaves his culture, leaves a place where his ancestors have probably lived for hundreds of years, to go off into a completely unknown territory where there are untamed natives threatening them – who takes this giant step in order to lead a new life? A self-selected collection of rugged individualists, for whom their own destiny was more important than staying in the comfort of their ancestral domains. It's true of the Quakers in Pennsylvania. It's true of the Catholics in Maryland. It's true of the Puritans in New England. It's true of Roger Williams in Providence, who couldn't stand what the Puritans next door did and ran away from them. It's true right down the line. And they bring with them the concepts of freedom that allowed them to depart in the first place – the idea that there's something to parliamentary democracy, the idea that people ought to rule themselves. But what they bring most of all is the determination to make a new life for themselves in a new world.

Once that begins, America becomes a haven for people like that from all over the world. That's what sets the tone. Think about it. Think about all the waves of immigration. These were waves of individuals. Every one of the people in those waves from all of those countries had to pick themselves up and uproot themselves from their communities, from their homes, from their friends. They went to an unknown world. They had no idea what they would see, who would help them. There was no safety net. They came over here with one determination: "I am going to make a new life for myself in a new world, however hard it may be." Anyone who has read the history of American immigration knows how hard it actually was. That doesn't seem to have stopped anybody from coming over. All the hardships here were as nothing compared to the determination of that self-selected group of people from all over the world who came over here to realize their personal dreams.

That is the reason for the unique form of democracy we have in this country. To be sure, it's a country that was set up on the basis of the English love of liberty and the English love of democracy. But the heart of it was a population that came over determined to empower itself and to make its own way in the new world.

The economic reality of the country fitted this framework perfectly. Until the middle of the nineteenth century, we were primarily an agricultural country. Over 90% of the people lived on individual farms. They homesteaded and they kept going West, because they wanted their own land. They were ruggedly individualistic farmers. Indeed, that was Jefferson's ideal: an America built on a solid foundation of small farmers who understand the role of individual empowerment.

You all know that in the 19th century, when the industrial era came of age, these ideals were severely tested. Industrialism inherently contradicts the idea of personal empowerment, because in the industrial era people had to become parts of machines, and the only way you can get people to become mechanized is to dehumanize them, to disempower them. That's why, throughout the industrial era in this country, there was a deep conflict between the economic system, which lost its agrarian character, and the fundamental American ideals. That conflict set the stage for all the major social battles of the late 19th century and early 20th century.

Today, the post-industrial age is here. We're at a point where the economic realities can once again, today and as in generations past, realize the ideal of empowerment, albeit in a non-agrarian setting.

What's true of American society today is true of the school. The school is basically about democracy as empowerment. Once you realize it, you see it everywhere. Let me read you what two former students said: "At first I was scared of the School Meeting, afraid somebody would ask me to say something and I wouldn't even know what to say. I went anyway, just because I was interested. I wanted to listen. L. was the

Chairman. I had read in books about how meetings were conducted with minutes and agendas and a Chairman and everything like that, but it was my first experience with a structured meeting. At first I was confused about L. I didn't know if he was a student or staff. When I found out he was a student, I was impressed. I thought he did a great job and I really admired him for doing it and looked up to him. I was amazed that one boy who was younger than me, he was nine or ten, spoke right up. I think he had been disciplined and he was trying to explain why he had done something. He just stood right up and spoke his piece. I was so amazed that he had no fear at all. It turned out that he had a good reason for what had happened and everyone ended up rescinding his sentence." Or the second quote: "Feeling equal is so important. That's the whole thing. As a kid it's extremely important because you feel like you have some authority and that you can express your feelings and somebody is going to listen to you. If somebody just throws a rule or something at you, it's almost like a natural reaction to want to rebel against it, but if you have something to do with it, if you're part of the decisions to make the rules, that whole democracy feeling, the situation is an advantage. I'm talking now as an adult, but as a kid I was aware of it. I knew that I had certain powers. 'Hey, we voted for staff.' You knew you had powers to vote people in, vote people out."

You see that every day in the school. It's absolutely gripping. There are a lot of issues that come up in the school and are matters of deep concern to a lot of members of the community. As far as I'm concerned, there is nothing more moving, more interesting, and more impressive than watching the School Meeting assemble, week after week, occasionally moving up to the barn when there isn't enough room, because one is witnessing the coming together of people who feel they have the power to affect their destinies and to make their opinions count. That doesn't mean that everybody gets their way. I certainly don't always get mine. Nobody always gets theirs. But the school provides the opportunity to try to realize your dreams through direct personal action.

Sudbury Valley gives hands-on experience, not simply in democratic government, but in the individual empowerment which is the core of the American democratic concept.

Developing Each Child's Unique Destiny:
Age Mixing, Positive and Negative Role Models, and Personal Independence

We always felt that Sudbury Valley was the best place to develop each child's unique potential to the fullest. That was a given for us from day one. The question is, how does this beautiful concept relate to setting up a school? It turns out that, when you think of the notion of developing each child's unique destiny, you realize that it connects directly into the great debate of Nature *vs.* nurture. And the fact is that, at least in this juncture in human history, no one has an answer to the question of which of these is the determining factor, or the most important factor, or what relative weight can be given to each one. Both factors seem to play a role. So, for us, the question became, how does the school environment relate to each of these two factors, assuming that they both play a role? How does the school environment help each child to realize their own destiny, whether you consider that destiny to be determined by Nature or by nurture?

Let's consider Nature first. The argument is that a child's potential and capabilities are largely determined by his/her genetic makeup. It's something inherent in the child from birth. The idea is that each child is born with a certain innate configuration that gets actuated as the child matures into adulthood – like hair color, or physical build. To the extent that this is true, then, the way to maximize a child's ability to realize his/her own destiny is to let Nature take its course! It seems pretty obvious once you focus on what it means. If there's a component of your destiny that's inherent, the best way to assure that it will be realized is to let Nature do its thing undisturbed. That should happen without barriers, and with the patience necessary to let the natural processes unfold.

That idea is the origin of the school's "Art of Doing Nothing" concept, which was first introduced in an article that Hanna wrote about twenty years ago[8]. The idea is not so much that you're doing nothing as that you're stepping aside and letting Nature do *something*. In other words, outsiders – staff, or parents, or other members of the school community – have to

---

[8] *The Sudbury Valley School Experience*, 3rd ed. (Sudbury Valley School Press; Framingham, 1992), p. 81ff.

take great care not to intervene in this natural unfolding of the child's capabilities. That's very important to us in the school. It has been for a long time. It's become reinforced by our experience over and over again. We have come to understand clearly that any intervention engaged in by the school will undermine, to a certain extent, the innate natural drives and tendencies of a growing child.

When we talked about the role of parents, we discussed how important it was for a parent, before intervening, to weigh the benefits of the intervention *vs.* the costs of the intervention. In the school environment, which is very different from the parental one, the excuses for intervening are less. In the school, our goal, to let the child's natural inclinations unfold, has to be uncompromised. We must exercise total restraint from putting up barriers or trying to direct the flow of the child's development.

There's a beautiful poem that came to my attention from Mary Oliver's book *Dreamwork*[9] that I would like to cite in this connection. It focuses on the damage that intervention can do to the natural unfolding. It's called "The Journey":

---

[9] (Atlantic Monthly Press: New York, 1986), p. 38.

*One day you finally knew
what you had to do, and began,
though the voices around you
kept shouting
their bad advice –
though the whole house
began to tremble
and you felt the old tug
at your ankles.
"Mend my life!"
each voice cried.
But you didn't stop.
You knew what you had to do,
though the wind pried
with its stiff fingers
at the very foundations –
though their melancholy
was terrible.
It was already late
enough, and a wild night,
and the road full of fallen
branches and stones.
But little by little,
as you left their voices behind,
the stars began to burn
through the sheets of clouds,
and there was a new voice,*

> *which you slowly*
> *recognized as your own,*
> *that kept you company*
> *as you strode deeper and deeper*
> *into the world,*
> *determined to do*
> *the only thing you could do –*
> *determined to save*
> *the only life you could save.*

One of the things that we gradually came to appreciate as we experienced this natural unfolding, was the crucial role *time* played in this drama. One of the most notable features of Sudbury Valley is the absence of time as a presence in the school. We don't have bells. There are no personal deadlines set for students by the school. Time, in the school, is treated as organic to the individual processes that each person undergoes. It's not a community concept. It's an individual concept. Each student in the school runs according to their own inner clock. That's something that any parent knows very well when they try to pick up their children! Even personal watches are seldom used during the day. It's because children understand that the rate at which the earth spins around its axis doesn't have anything to do with what happens inside them as human beings in their developing lives. For SVS to work, students and their families have to get accustomed to the fact that the tyranny of time has to be removed altogether.

This is something that the society around us finds very hard to accept. I'm not talking here about bells. The greatest tyranny of time that outside society imposes, and that the school avoids carefully, is the tyranny of developmental milestones. This is a curse that modern pseudoscience has introduced into the theory of natural human development. I can't really explain why, historically, this concept has become such a fad. When I was growing up, nobody talked about it; then, the accepted reality was, "It's never too late!" One of our heroes was Albert Schweitzer, one of the greatest organists in Europe, who in his mid-30's threw it all away to go to medical school and become a doctor, to follow his inner dream of medical service to Africa. For us, this was held out as a model. You can always change. It's never too late.

For some reason, just as the whole world has started to abandon the tyranny of time, the science of developmental psychology has fastened onto it as a fad. The conclusions that are drawn from the so-called scientific experiments that are done in this area are based on scanty material which is poorly understood, and can only be characterized as a leap of imagination. Yet, a lot of parents are very nervous when they hear that if their child doesn't learn a second language by the age of X, then their ability to learn a second language is gone. If they don't have mathematical skills by the age of Y, then they'll never be good at mathematics. There's a whole slew of these statements that are supposedly backed up by studies. Whenever I look at these studies – brain waves, CAT scans, statistical analyses, etc. – I always think of the ant. I think of this tiny insect, which has nothing that you would really call a brain. It has complex behavior that we have no clue about. We have no idea how the ant's cognition works, whatever that means. When I think of that, I say, "This fad, too, will pass, because we certainly are not going to understand the alleged milestones in the development of the human brain before we understand how an ant's brain works."

We have to be free of the tyranny of externally imposed life timetables as well. The tyranny of saying, "You should be out of here when you're 18. You should be starting to study for your SAT's when you're 16." These are milestones externally imposed by families, and by society. These, too, run counter to the natural inner development of each child. We've learned this very well over the past thirty years. Some people are ready to graduate or go out into the world at age 16. Some people aren't ready until they're 20 or 21. In the long run it makes no difference. When lifespans were

25 or 30 years, you might have had an argument for, "Get with it by the age of 13." People got married at 13 or 14. You have to get a perspective on this. Chopin wrote his first piano concerto at the age of 19. You say, "Oh my God, I'm 20 and I haven't done a damn thing," and you start feeling that life has passed you by. That's absurd. Chopin had to get on with his life. He was dead by 36. He may not have known that he'd be dead by 36 when he was 19, but people all over were dying at 36. So he might have guessed. Our lifespan is 70, 75, 80, who knows? No rush. For the Nature part to unfold, the tyranny of time has to go away.

But there is an other aspect of time, which it took us much longer to appreciate. That was the significance of *the present*. It's one thing to realize that you don't have to worry about time spans, but quite another to appreciate the present moment. One of the beautiful things about children is their ability to immerse themselves totally in the present. There's no question – and certainly Eastern philosophy has accentuated this – that fully appreciating the beauty and complexity and richness of the present moment, with all of its nuances, letting it flood into you, is an enormously enriching experience that does much to open up your inner potential. Adults in industrial and urban societies have mostly gotten away from that. The present has been almost too difficult to bear, and so the present has been pushed aside. Instead, people tended to concentrate on the future, even on an afterlife. The present was just too miserable to contemplate.

In a school like Sudbury Valley, where time isn't a factor, children don't lose that ability to love and appreciate the present. You can see that in the adult graduates of the school as they grow up. You watch them in their twenties, in their thirties, in their forties by now. One of the things you see and marvel at about these people is they haven't lost the ability to revel in the beauty of the present. That I find to be one of the most significant aspects of how the school has enriched the Nature part of each person's search for their destiny.

Let's turn now to the nurture component, which is a little more complicated. Understanding how the nurture aspect of development affects each child's march to his or her destiny is critical when setting up a school, because a school is, by definition, an environment. If you are concerned about how the environment nurtures the child, you've got to be extremely sensitive to everything you put into that environment.

I'd like to pause briefly to discuss the various environments in which a child grows up. The most visible one is the larger culture, American culture in our case. They are immersed in that culture. We don't have anything to do with that as a school because, living in America, they can't get away from their American environment. The only way to avoid it is by moving somewhere else. A lot of parents don't like certain aspects of the American environment. My message to them is, don't fight city hall. You can't avoid the fact that this is America. You can move to Australia. You can move to the Middle East. But if you're stuck in this country, you're going to have children who grow up in American culture, and the only thing that you're going to achieve by fighting it is getting the kids to want to know more than ever what it is that you're keeping from them.

We've seen this in our own family, with our children and TV. Our kids were born in the sixties and, like so many of our contemporaries, we did not want to expose them to TV. We kept it in the closet after we finally bought it. The kids would ask every now and then, "What's that thing that looks like a suitcase?" and we wouldn't answer – until we finally realized that what they were doing, of course, was spending an awful lot of time at their friends' houses, looking at TV! When I was a child, I wasn't allowed to read comic books, and guess what I did in my spare time? I went to my friends' houses and read comic books!

You can't fight it. What happened was that the minute we said to our first child, "Ok, you can have TV," he sat in front of the tube all day, just to show us. After a while, he decided there were other things in life. Our youngest child, who had TV around from day one, hardly looked at it. You can't avoid the culture you're immersed in. You can exert your own influences. You can say what you think about it. There's nothing stopping you from giving your opinions, but the ambient culture is everywhere, and it's unavoidable.

Then there's the culture of the family's wider social circle, which includes the religious groups that you might belong to, or the social groups, or the business groups. This is a kind of sub-culture, and the child grows up in that too, and is deeply influenced by it. If you reminisce about your childhood, you will surely have many memories from this wider social circle – from your synagogue, or church, or youth group. These are all part of the environmental nurturing that affect a person's upbringing.

The other major environment is the family, with which I have already dealt[10]. It is, in many ways, the strongest influence on a child as s/he grows up, as we have discussed at length.

---

[10] "What *Is* the Role of Parents?", above.

Compared to these three environments – the larger culture, the wider social sub-culture, and the family culture – the school seems to play a pretty minor role. It's just a place that kids go to for a certain number of hours a day, every weekday during the school year, which turns out to be half of the year, 180 days or so. It doesn't sound like very much, except that it *is*! And the reason it is very much is that the school is the only environment children experience where they are directly exposed, on a regular basis, to people with whom they're not familiar. This turns out to be critical. The school is a model of the situation that will face children when they become adults. Think how odd, and terrifying, and strange it is to a student to come into the school for the first time! Here you are, in a place where you're destined to spend many long hours, surrounded by people whom you don't know at all. These are people you are going to encounter every day, face to face, interacting with them, watching them interact. It's a microcosm of the "real world" of adults. Children are aware of this, and when adults tell children that school is the place that prepares them for the adult world, they are on the mark, at least from the perspective I have been discussing.

If we understand the school to be a crucial environment because it's a model of the larger world, the question becomes, "What's the best school environment that we can create to nurture each child to realize their full potential and unique destiny?" How do we design it? What kinds of things should a child be exposed to in order to maximize the likelihood of realizing their unique destiny? That's the question you're putting to yourself when you discuss the creation of a school.

The answer given by traditional schools is straightforward. They say the nurturing exposure that you need is to a certain specific grouping of content and skills. Given that exposure, they maintain that children will develop so that, in the end, they'll be able to find their way in life. The specific skills and content chosen by educators are the ones they consider to be necessary for every adult to have to function in the modern world.

We've talked about this a lot in our writings. There are two things wrong with this notion, which we never, ever considered as a factor in creating our environment. The first thing wrong is that anything of that sort must involve active intervention. The idea of an environment that exposes children to a given set of skills or content *requires* intervention on the part of the adults. This, as we have seen, runs against the natural tendency of the child to develop in his/her own way. You cannot avoid that friction, and that is the source of the resistance that every schoolchild develops, in one form or another, to school – even kids who like school, as I did. You may like it, but you resent being forced into it because it's contrary to human nature.

The second problem is determining what group of skills and content people should be exposed to. Nobody can agree on this. In fact, agreement is impossible in the post-industrial Information Age. So, what you get is groups of people creating ever more comprehensive lists of things that every child has to know.

I have a big book, which weighs about fifteen pounds and has 650 pages in it. It is a compendium of standards and benchmarks for K-12 education. This book represents the thinking of the best educators in this country, as of 1998, as to what it is that *every child in this country* should know before they graduate high school in order to function effectively in the world. This is the required exposure we have been talking about.

Now, when I grew up, the book probably had 30 pages in it. But the world became more complex, and as the world became more complex the response was to keep adding more and more topics to cover the complexity. I don't have the space to entertain you with the contents of this book, but almost anywhere that you turn you find an absurd example. I'll just open this thing at random to show a typical example: "It's essential that every child in grades five to six in the country" — don't lose sight of this, this is not specialized, this isn't for Boston Latin or Bronx High School of Science, this is for *every* child, *everywhere* – "must understand the impact of European military and commercial involvement in Asia, e.g. how the Netherlands, England and France became naval and commercial powers in the Indian Ocean Basin in the 17th and 18th centuries. The impact of British and French commercial and military penetration on politics, economy and society in India. Why the Dutch wanted military and commercial influence in Indonesia and how this imperialism affected the region's economy in society." This is *one item* for grades five to six!

In case you think that was unusual, there's a whole section here for grades five to six, and seven to eight, and nine to twelve, three whole pages of subject matter "which assures that everybody in those grades will have an understanding of the major developments in east Asia and southeast Asia in the era of the Tang dynasty from 600 to 900." These are the Goals 2000 announced by President Bush and fervently pursued by both political parties. The only thing they compete about is who can put more pages into the book and whether the test should be national, which of course the Democrats want, or whether every state should develop its own book, which the Republicans want. It makes for a lot more books!

So, the question is, what should the school environment provide if it doesn't provide that? What is the environment that *is* best for nurturing children to their unique paths in life? The way we've come to understand it, that environment should meet three criteria.

First of all, anything in the environment must be universally useful in later life. Second, it must be related to basic human drives and characteristics. It can't run counter to natural inclinations. It has to run *with* nature, not against nature. Thus, whatever it is that you put into the environment, it has to be useful in a relatively passive way. It has to be there to be used, not imposed, because it has to be accessible and desired by the child naturally and not the result of an active intervention that breeds resistance. The third criterion is that it has to be essential to each child's quest to realize their unique destiny.

If you look at those three criteria, there aren't a lot of things that satisfy them. In fact, as far as we can see, the only thing that really satisfies all three is something that gives children practice in *thinking about things* – in figuring out how the world works, and in problem solving. These are skills that everyone has, by Nature. Everybody is born with the ability to think, with the ability to figure out the world around them. What you want to do in the school's environment is provide something in the environment that will give that inborn skill a lot more use and practice in a natural way, without intervention. Not by teaching people how to think. Not by setting up courses in logical thinking. But by creating something in the environment that will naturally enhance the ability of children to think and solve problems.

Over the years, we came to realize what that "something" is. It's the concept of the *role model* in its broadest sense in the school – a passive example provided by other people in the school for the child to observe with respect to how they behave and how they think. Perhaps the most important way children and adults perfect their thinking skills is by watching and figuring out how other people think. We saw in an earlier talk, about conversation, that the desire to watch how other people figure out the world is at the root of why children want to communicate all the time, because the essence of that communication is to find out how other people think.

The greater the range of role models available in the school and accessible to children, the more useful the environment, the more helpful it will be to enhancing a child's ability to solve problems. That is the reason that age mixing is such a central feature of the school. Age mixing is the mechanism through which effective modeling takes place in the school. Age mixing comes in two varieties. I want to talk about them briefly so that you'll get a picture of how rich the age mixing is in the school and how important it is in the environment.

The first is age mixing within a relatively narrow range of a few years: six year olds mixing with kids between the age of four and eight, for example. The value of that kind of narrow range age mixing was probably first appreciated most fully by a person whose name has become somewhat familiar, the Russian psychologist Lev Vygotsky, who developed for that concept the term "zone of proximal development". He found that children challenge themselves constantly by interacting within this zone of proximal development, within this range of skills that are fairly close to their own. They stretch their minds by advancing to a point just a little beyond their reach, but tantalizingly close enough so that they are able to work hard to get there. The six year old admires the eight year old for all that the eight year old has achieved. But the eight year old is not so far out of range that the six year old can't see him/herself there. So they try. And it's worth trying because, even though there's a lot of failure involved, failure, and overcoming failure, are part of what makes the process work.

The benefit works in the other direction, too, which is very important to understand. What eight year olds get out of interacting with six year olds is a consolidation of their gains. That's thoroughly understanding where you've come from. That's saying to yourself, "I used to do that, but now I know better." It's the kind of thing that a teacher gets from teaching. Everybody knows that when you teach something, you learn it so much better. When you model for somebody just a little younger than you, you're consolidating where you are. You're entrenching yourself in your thinking skills. Then you look at ten year olds, in turn, and you stretch to them, while the ten year olds are looking at you and doing the same consolidation, and the same stretching to the twelve year olds! You see this in Sudbury Valley all the time, everywhere. You see it in the kitchen. You see it in the art room. You see it in the music room. You see it in chess, in games, in 4-square – everywhere, interaction within the zone of proximal development is an important part of life.

The second type of age mixing that happens in the school occurs over a broad range of ages. It took us a while to appreciate the value of this. Wide range age mixing gives children something different; it gives them insight into how adults work. A puzzle in itself. It's not so much that they're figuring out the next step for themselves, as they do in the zone of proximal development, but they're trying to understand, "When I grow up, what's it going to be like?" Which is an answer every kid wants to know. So they watch older people and how they do things. Kids study older people in detail.

Recently, I was talking to a group of people at a sister Sudbury school. There were kids present. I happened to be touching on this subject, and it was really very amusing. I said, "Kids know their parents better than anybody does." All the kids shook their heads in agreement, and all the parents looked at them daggers. But, it's true. Kids know us. The kids in the school study the staff. The kids know the foibles, the weaknesses, the strengths of the staff members much better than we adults know our colleagues. They've got us totally figured out. This is a key part of that role modeling, to figure out, "How do adults do it?" What could be a more useful environment for getting ready for the adult world?

Here is how one former student (now a staff member) put it:

> *In previous schools, I'd walk into a classroom and a teacher would already be sitting behind a desk and would deliver whatever it was they had to deliver for 45 minutes for a year, two years, however long they had to teach it, and then I would move on. The teacher would park someplace, another part of the campus. The*

teacher would eat on another part of the campus. The teacher would speak outside of the range of the student's hearing. I came to Sudbury Valley and it was fascinating to see what kind of vehicles, bicycles, motorcycles, cars, whatever, the staff were driving. It was fascinating to see that they would sit and eat lunch and I could sit next to them and watch what they ate, and how they ate, if they had good table manners. How many different clothes they would wear and how they would dress in the cold and whether they wore hats or not. As a fifteen year old kid, I really had not spent time around grownups at work before. I'd occasionally get to go with my dad to the shop or see my mother and her friends around the table, but to come here and see adults at work every day, you really get to see how they lived and you could pick up so much in that real-life setting. It was tremendous role modeling and I took away so much from that.

The beauty of the school's lack of tenure is that when the school community concludes that there isn't enough value to the role modeling that they get from a staff member, they remove him/her from their midst. What you might perceive as a value or I might perceive as a value does not necessarily correspond with what somebody else might see as a value. They might see, in that particular person, a modeling of some character features, for example, or some conversational abilities that I can't see. I might even vote "no" for that person whereas fifty other people might vote "yes". There's a mechanism here for constantly reviewing and renewing the role models in the school. And, of course, the student role models change all the time because students come and go.

What do adults at school get out of it? That's a question I used to ask myself for a long time. I used to wonder, how come, here it is 30 years later and I'm not burned out? Why? Because the older people refresh their own innocence, their wide-eyed lust for knowledge and life, by looking at the littler kids. You can see that happening with the teenagers, not only with the adults. The teenagers are constantly interacting with the little kids, and this interaction keeps the child in them alive. This is especially important in the teenage years, which are the worst years to live through. You're not supposed to be a child anymore. "When I was a child I spake as a child, but now I'm supposed to set aside all these childish things. What does all this mean? Do I really have to grow up and become like my parents and like all these other adults?" It's a horrible time of life, and here at Sudbury Valley you are surrounded by, and in direct contact with, children who are bouncy and full of life and full of mischief, and it keeps the child in you alive – that ability to be creative, to be imaginative, not to be tied down by convention, not to be tied down about all those things that you worry about on a daily basis.

Role models can be positive or negative. Negative role models are just as important as positive ones. This became really clear to us years ago when our oldest son reached his teenage years. One day, out of the blue, he said, "Those two years that I spent as a kid, when I was about seven or eight years old, in the smoking room back in '68 and '69, were the best years ever for me." At the time, in '68 and '69, when we saw our seven year old hanging out in the smoking room with all the beatniks, we wondered. Our son said something very simple: "This period was wonderful. It taught me what I wanted to emulate, because these people were phenomenal musicians. They had lots of imagination. They were fun. They were interesting. And it taught me what I didn't want to do. I saw how drugs, for example, wrecked them, and drugs just never interested me after that." Now, other children might reach other conclusions, but the point I'm making is that the negative role model that these kids see is of crucial importance to their development. Kids can look at an adult and say, "I don't want to be like that person. I don't want to be irritable. I don't want to be narrow-minded. I don't want to have this or that trait, or behave in this or that manner." Kids don't have a chance to think that way if they aren't exposed to wide range age mixing.

I want to address briefly a paradox that might have occurred to you. I'm talking about each child realizing their own unique destiny and developing something that's very much their own. How, then, does that gibe with role modeling, which seems to involve copying somebody else? We often hear that from parents: "I'm worried about my child. She seems to be aping everything that X is doing. Is this good? What shall I do about it? I don't like the fact that she's following X around and doing everything that X says." There is no real paradox in that once you understand that a child who feels really empowered, a child who feels really in control of his/her own destiny, is not slavishly *following* the role model. They're *studying* the role model. The more role models there are for them to study intensely in their environment, the more options they open for themselves in later life. As long as you have trust and confidence that your child is developing their own inner voice, you don't have to worry about how much they copy someone else at some stage of their development.

Finally, I want to touch on something that I brushed aside. When I showed you the big, thick book, I begged the question: "How do kids find out about the world? How do they find out about the stuff – some of the stuff, at least – in that book?" Here, age mixing plays a key role as well. We all know how much people are inundated with information from TV and from movies, but age mixing is a much more important source of information. Children, in the course of the days and weeks and months that they interact with each other and talk to each other and exchange ideas with each other, over this broad and narrow age range, talk about just about everything. They hear about everything. The likelihood of their coming across something that really excites them is very, very high.

Why Sudbury Valley School Doesn't Work for Everyone:
Real Learning Disabilities

During our founding years, we thought that people would flock to the school. We thought we would be mobbed and we'd be turning people away at the door. We expected a cast of thousands. Who wouldn't want happy kids? More to the point, what kids wouldn't do everything in their power to gain their freedom? We expected, even if the parents weren't willing, that the kids would be knocking down the walls, making their parents' lives miserable. "Send us to Sudbury Valley, or we'll go on a hunger strike." We were very quickly disabused, and instead we underwent a long struggle to survive, to grow, to gain acceptance.

It's a fact that the whole idea of the school started spreading to other places only during our third decade. The question we were always asked in those first twenty years was, "If it's such a great idea, how come everybody isn't doing it? How come there are no other schools like this one?" I had an answer, but not in my heart. I didn't really know why. It took us a good two decades to become respectable in the educational community, to become accepted as a legitimate educational enterprise. We struggled to understand why it was so hard.

We weren't naive. We understood that cultural changes don't happen overnight. There have only been a handful of major cultural changes in human history. The shift from hunter/gatherer societies to urban society took hundreds, perhaps thousands, of years. The shift from a pre-industrial to an industrial society took over a hundred years. These things take time. We were not ignorant of history. But we thought that the reason most shifts took time was that they ran counter to human nature. The hunter/gatherer state was a state of relative freedom, of a certain kind of relationship with the environment and with oneself. We felt that's the natural evolved human condition, so to shift from that, in a counter-evolutionary way, to urban living, or from an urban pre-industrial society to an industrial society – that's hard. That's why there's resistance. Societies had to figure out if the tradeoff was worth it, if the benefits were worth the cost. In each case society made those major shifts only after struggling to understand that the benefits outweighed the costs. For example, the benefit in going to an urban society was a certain amount of stability – political stability, safety, shelter, a more dependable food supply, a more organized social order. So society gave up its freedom in order to have certain things that enabled people to live in a way that was, overall, more satisfactory. That's why efforts to save hunter/gatherer societies today are all basically doomed to failure; Indians living in the Amazonian rainforest can resist the tradeoff only so long before they realize that there are benefits to living in an urban setting that they don't have. Similarly, we all know that the wrenching transition from a pre-industrial to an industrial society was almost a Faustian deal. Society lost even more freedom, but gained material benefits that were never dreamt of before, available to a much larger segment of the community than ever before.

We thought, "That's why these changes took so long. That's the reason for the resistance." But here we were talking about a transition from an industrial to a post-industrial age, which goes *with* evolution, which is *consistent* with human nature. We thought, "When we create a suitable educational environment for the post-industrial age, people should heave a sigh of relief, because finally they'll be able to act naturally." I remember using a phrase over and over again in the first ten or fifteen years, because it was so real to me: "Now you can have your cake and eat it too!" I thought, who wouldn't like to have his cake and eat it too? People can enjoy all the benefits that they had all along, even more so in post-industrial society, and they can also have the freedom that they had to give up way, way back in pre-history, when they gave up their original relatively free state of Nature. We thought people would respond eagerly to that. That's why we thought the change would occur fairly rapidly.

It was only much more recently that we realized that our problem was really part of a larger global ecological problem – namely, the difficulty of restoring the natural balance once it has been ravaged.

People have come to understand this pretty well in environmental studies. If you have forests that have been clear cut, rivers that have been contaminated, oceans that have been rid of their fish and polluted, land that has been poisoned by toxic chemicals, we have learned that it takes decades, perhaps even centuries, to recover, even if you allow them to revert to their natural condition. It's not enough simply to suddenly stop the ecological degradation. In conservation circles, there's a great deal of discussion about ways to restore the natural balance. One method that is receiving a great deal of attention is to pick small environments to restore first. Conservation societies are buying a few hundred acres here, a few thousand there, and trying to accumulate a patchwork of small areas that might be amenable to restoration. They look for areas relatively close to their natural state, which are difficult to find. You cannot go anywhere just at random, put your finger on a map, and say, "I'm going to buy a million acres here and I'm going to make this into a great, wonderful, pure, natural preserve." If that million acres happens to be a Superfund area, you can't do it. So you have to look for small areas that are already somewhat in sync with nature, and the hope is that gradually people will see what it looks like for nature to be restored to its pristine beauty and come to say, "This is something we really want. Let's do more of it. Let's change our life pattern so that we, too, can be surrounded by a beautiful natural environment."

In a sense, what we learned is that *we have to view Sudbury Valley as a cultural restoration program.* We have to realize that not every person is in a position to benefit from this because of the damage that's been done by urbanization and industrialization. That's when we began to understand why we had to start with a very small number of people. It's inevitable. The people we had to start with are the ones who are somehow more in touch with their naturally evolved state. Slowly, we would add a group here and a group there in the hope that, eventually, people would see that these little restoration projects that happen all over the country, or all over the world, are something that they want to adopt and emulate.

That picture gives you a perspective on what's happening. That's the basis for two questions that I want to address. The first one is, "Why are so few people still adapted to their natural state? What is the nature of the damage that's been done – culturally, emotionally, psychologically, and intellectually – that so alienates people from their natural state?" The second question, which I'll address later, is: "Who are those few people who are able to benefit from this environment?"

Let's begin with the question, "What's the nature of the damage?" Or, stated another way, "What are *real* learning disabilities, things that *really* stand in the way of people adapting to their natural evolutionary state?" It shouldn't come as a surprise that the material of the first five talks gives the framework for the answer.

Let's consider the first subject we talked about, play. We talked at length about the importance of play – how crucial, how central play is to the natural development of all the skills that are important to a creative life. Yet, over and over again, we find that kids coming to Sudbury Valley have forgotten how to play. This is an absolutely staggering phenomenon. For example, young kids are the ones you really expect to be able to romp freely, to do their thing, to be joyous. Yet, occasionally we see young kids who have no idea how to play! When we get to know them a little better, we see that what they learned at home, or from some other environment, was that play is something *directed* – the *opposite* of what play really means. Play has become, for them, what commercial and educational groups have turned it into: something oriented in a visibly educational direction. They have to learn their alphabet from play, their shapes from play, their colors from play. I could never understand any of this when I first encountered it; and when I saw the damage it does to kids, it became even more amazing. Why do you have to teach kids shapes? What is going on? What child who has grown up in even the most remotely normal environment doesn't figure out at some age or another that there's a difference between a square and a triangle, and what that difference is. What child (who isn't color blind) doesn't eventually learn that something is called red and something else is called blue? Do we really have to create games for which that is the goal? We get kids who have been brought up on that, and they come to our school, and they're at a loss because we're not doing it. They've simply forgotten how to play freely.

With older kids, it's even more sad. The whole point is to retain that ability to play throughout life. Older kids, however, have been taught to "put aside childish things." They're embarrassed about the idea of play. A lot of teenagers will look at the younger kids who are playing and tell you, "Gee, I wish I had come here when I was seven"; and you know exactly what they mean. Some of them will start playing with the little kids, which they feel is OK, because they're "being nice to little kids," so that justifies it. In reality, they're trying to learn how to play again themselves. That's a terrible disability, when you've forgotten how to play. Anybody who's forgotten how to play cannot begin to comprehend how an environment like Sudbury Valley is a school, how it has anything to do with education. They can't possibly take it seriously. That's the first thing you hear, "Is this a school? People play all day!" They don't get it, because they've forgotten how to play, and they've never had a chance to realize the tremendous benefit that play gives you.

Let's turn to conversation. Sometimes, children come to the school who are almost mute. They just don't talk. It's not shyness. It's a response to something they've been told all their lives: children should be seen and not heard. "Shut up!" is probably something that's been said to children more than any other two words. At school? You're *never* supposed to talk to other students at school! You get demerits if you talk to your neighbor in class. You can't get up out of your seat and talk to somebody on the other side of the room. You certainly can't talk to the teacher whenever you please, because that's disrupting the class, unless you're answering a specific question. You're not supposed to speak unless spoken to. As a result, many children never learn how to converse, how to tap into somebody else's world, to probe it, to appreciate it, to listen, to share their own world with others. Children in that position tend to be closed in on themselves. They have to reinvent the wheel. They have to discover everything on their own. It's like being cut off from the culture.

Conversation is, as we have seen, a tremendous key to learning. It's that "open sesame" that relates you to global knowledge. People who don't have the ability to converse and to articulate their thoughts are at a tremendous disadvantage in an environment like Sudbury Valley. They can't use one of our most important tools. I'm not talking about children who are naturally reserved. I'm not talking about children who know that there's a time to talk and a time to listen, who sometimes just keep quiet and watch what's going on. I'm talking about children who really haven't learned how to converse. For children like that, the vibrant atmosphere of the school is sometimes absolutely frightening. What you encounter as soon as you walk into the school is a cacophony of live, vibrant conversation. The child who cannot converse doesn't benefit from that at all.

We talked a lot about the parental role. That's another huge area for potential damage. Kids whose chief motivation is pleasing their parents don't know how to please themselves. They don't know how to tap into their inner voice. They're looking to see what is it that their parents really want them to do in this school, and they try to do that, with the result that they miss the whole point of the school. We see that in so many different ways, some so subtle and seemingly so harmless. The parent who leads their younger child to the bulletin board and says, "Let's see what's posted here today" – there doesn't seem anything wrong with that. "My kid can't read and I'm helping him see what's going on." But actually, there's a lot wrong with that. You're signaling to your child, "I don't really trust you to find out for yourself what's going on in this place." In reality, even the youngest children know what's going on in the place when they care about it. They can recite half the Lawbook. They can't read, but they can tell you that there's no running, no abuse of property, no this, no that. They know what their sentences are. They can smell the smells coming out of the kitchen and they can see the other kids going skating. They're not deaf, dumb and blind. But the combination of parental anxiety and the desire to please the parent suffuses that little interaction at the bulletin board, and the kid goes away feeling, "I should be doing this. If I did this, I'd make my mom real happy."

With older children, we get that all the time with classes. I'm not talking about the parent who stomps in like a bull in a china shop and flatly says, "I want you to take classes at school." That's beyond the pale. I'm talking about the parent who is gently inquiring, "Have you found anything interesting going on in the school?" Or, more commonly, "You're interested in so and so. Have you found somebody in school to do that with?" Innocently, thinking: "I'm not pushing. I'm just asking." My mother would always say, "I'm only asking." But I knew she wasn't asking. She was telling me exactly what she wanted. We get a similar problem with children trying to please parents when we have two parents in a family who are conflicted about the school. It's perfectly legitimate for a person to say, "I don't think Sudbury Valley is the right environment." That's a right any parent has, to say this is or isn't good for my kid. But when a child is in a family where one parent is saying, "I'm behind the school and I think it's a wonderful place," and the other parent is saying, "I really have my doubts about the place. I'll go along with it, but I sure hope I see some progress" – that kind of conflict will tear a student apart; not only is there the problem of pleasing parents in general, but s/he doesn't even know which parent to please. Something like that often crops up in families where one child goes to Sudbury Valley and the other children don't, especially if the reason, as we so often hear, is that "He (or she) is the only one who is having problems. The others are doing fine." There's only one possible message that a child can get from that. "If I was OK like my brothers and sisters, I wouldn't be here. This isn't a place where what goes on is really learning. I've just been parked here because I can't do the right thing." Many of these children are plagued by a nagging sense of having failed their parents. That's a terrible thing to carry through life.

Let's talk about democratic empowerment. Almost all the children who come to Sudbury Valley, even the youngest kids, have had other outside experiences where they have suffered from a lack of respect. The fact of the matter is that in society at large, kids are treated like dirt. It can be at the shopping mall, it can be driving on the road, it can be at a party, it can be in school – anywhere. Kids are non-people in a very real sense. They don't have rights, and they can be abused in many ways without consequence. The more original and creative, the more maverick, the more full of life the child is, the more likely s/he'll be treated with disrespect, because s/he doesn't even have the "courtesy" of going along with the standards that the adults want them to obey.

This is something that was almost impossible for me to understand when we first opened in 1968. I remember many conversations about it. I couldn't comprehend why children who were given full respect and equality in the school, who were completely empowered from the word "go", still *felt* powerless. I just couldn't get it. When they would try to explain it, I would say, "But that's the past. It's not like that here. I don't have power over you. I can't tell you what to do. Even if I want to, even if I stand over you and I say, 'Do this,' you could look at me and say, 'I don't want to do it,' because I don't have that kind of authority. This is an environment in which you have full respect and in which you are empowered." They couldn't let go of that deep feeling of powerlessness with which they had first arrived. Year in, year out, it leads to a kind of "us *vs.* them" mentality, especially in older teenagers, where they just can't help feeling: "This is a hoax. There's something fishy about it. There must be a hidden agenda. I don't know what it is. But I know in my bones that the adults must run this place. Somehow."

It's interesting and sad to watch this sense of powerlessness play itself out. For example, you can come to School Meetings where there is an issue that is really important to a lot of teenagers. The room will be packed with teenagers. So, you think, they're obviously coming to vote; they're participating in the democratic process this school developed and nurtured. And then, even as they talk and exercise their empowerment, *the content and the feeling of what they say is,* "We are powerless, and we resent the fact that somebody is trying to push something down our throats." It's inside them. It's a tremendous impediment. People who grow up feeling powerless are not going to go out into the world and be powerful adults.

This brings us to Nature *vs.* nurture, the subject that we took up most recently. I am referring to the damage that's been done to children who grow up in an environment where the adults have not let Nature take its course, have not been patient, and where each child's unique destiny has not been treasured as a valued life goal.

Now, that may be all very high-sounding, but in fact I talk to parent after parent who says to me, "My kids are not that special. They're not Einsteins or Mozarts. This kind of education may be OK for that type of person, but not for my kid." It's an expression of a basic parental belief that "My kid isn't really unique. My kid is mediocre." Such parents look at the life projected for that child of theirs as basically a life of drudgery, to be slogged through somehow.

I think this is the damage that we see most frequently at Sudbury Valley: kids who don't believe that they can do something really special with their lives, whatever it is – to excel at something that they love and to contribute in some way to the betterment of society, to the enhancement of culture, to their own personal joy. In many ways, that's the worst of the learning disabilities. What happens in that situation is that since you're destined for mediocrity, the pressure that is put on you by society, by your parents, by everybody, is to be a *successful* mediocrity. That's really important. You can at least be a comfortable drudge. There's time pressure, career pressure, expectations, a whole panoply of eternal forces. "Let's get on with it. Don't waste time. Focus on something. Go to school. Do this. Do that." It's pressure, pressure, pressure.

The most common result that we see of that kind of pressure is depression or anxiety, and a complete inability to be at peace with the concept that you should learn and do what you really want to learn, do what you really want to do, and follow your own star. I think the saddest example we see of this particular learning disability is the "A" student who excels in all of his/her studies. I myself am a lifelong recovering "A" student. When I think about all the energy I spent in validating someone else's concept of what's important to my destiny, it's just mind boggling. What on earth did I get A's in? What did I get 100's on tests for? They were inane. They had nothing to do with my life. They had nothing to do with reality. But there I was, slogging away, getting the first prize in Latin. The first prize in Latin! Do you know how useful that's been to me?[11]

Children totally focused on getting A's are like any person who's hooked on something, or who has a major problem: if they don't recognize the problem, and they're not ready to fight to free themselves of whatever

---

[11] I guess Latin is useful sometimes. Isaac Newton wrote a book when he was twenty-one, his first real production. It was a new theory of optics. It was a fabulous book. Physicists still read it with joy, and a lot of the ideas that he put into that book are still talked about. But they ran contrary to the accepted theories of optics in his day and, in particular, they ran contrary to the theories that his elders in the English physics establishment held to be sacrosanct. So he was lambasted for being an upstart, for not toeing the line, and he decided never to write another book. "I'm happy. I'm doing my thing. I know what I like." He had a professorship, so he didn't have to worry about his income, and he just sat in his place in Cambridge and did his stuff. Twenty years later the rumor got out that he had solved the problem of gravitation. So a couple of physicists who heard about this in London came up and said, "We heard that you solved the problem of gravitation. Is it true?" He said, "Yes, that's true." They said, "What is it?" He showed them. He wrote it out, and they were flabbergasted, because they immediately saw that he was right. They said, "Write it." He said, "I've done my writing for my lifetime." They begged him and begged him to write it, and he finally wrote it in a book called *Principia Mathematica*, which was written in Latin. The optics book had been written in everyday English. His new book was written in Latin that almost nobody could understand, and all the simple proofs that were easy to read he replaced with obscure proofs that were very difficult to follow. So perhaps I could have used my Latin. Maybe *Free at Last* should have been written in Latin! But I didn't.

it is that their problem is, somebody else can't do it for them. There's no point in lecturing them; they have to be ready to get themselves out of it. We've had some pretty remarkable situations like that over the years. One that comes to mind is the young lady who came to us at age 16 after having been a totally successful student in public school. She had decided that wasn't what she wanted. She was very conscious of this, and she left her high school career right in midstream. All she had to do was hang in there for another year and a half and she would have been out, but she wasn't ready to play along any more. She knew she had to save herself and she worked very, very hard during the two years that she was here. Did she get back to her natural evolutionary state? Probably not. But because of her intense desire to make a change, she did make huge strides.

It's important to distinguish between giving good grades and providing encouragement through positive feedback. The kind of positive feedback we're interested in is saying, "We're listening to you. We respect you. What you're doing is worthwhile because you want to do it." It's a whole different way of looking at things. We don't substitute our judgment for the child's judgment. What we give them instead is the consistent reply that what you do, what you value, is valuable *because you value it*, not because we think it's great.

There's a wonderful story in *Kingdom of Childhood*,[12] which is a book we publish consisting of reminiscences of former students. The student was on her visiting week when this happened. She entered the art room as a little four year old and drew a sun. The sun was green. She probably didn't get enough color training in her early play. She showed it to Joan. Joan's response wasn't, "That's an 'A' drawing," or "That's an 'F' drawing." It was, "That's fine! It's your drawing, and if that's the way you want to draw the sun, it's perfectly OK." She remembered that all her life because, being four and very smart, she was testing Joan on that first day to find out, "Is this another school like all the others? Is she going to tell me the sun is yellow and I don't know my colors?" So that's the kind of feedback they get: if they value it, it's fine. That's not always easy. If you walk into the sewing room on an average day, there are thirty people having three or four different very animated conversations. Some of the stuff these kids say is off the wall, having no relation to any reality whatsoever that I can detect. But there they are, going at it, this one sure of his point of view and

---

[12] (Sudbury Valley School Press; Framingham, 1994), p. 175.

that one sure of her point of view – and that's the point, that this is a place where they're each saying, "OK, if you want to have this world view, I'll listen to it. I'll interact with it, and I'll tell you mine, without us necessarily agreeing with each other." There is that fundamental respect for other ways of doing things.

That's the kind of feedback students get here. And they leave thinking, "I guess there is a place where what I do is valued for the fact that I do it and I want it." That's the gift we can give them.

The sad part of it is that the public school kids who are most creative, the kids who really, really don't care about school, who cannot pay attention to what their teachers are saying, who cannot tolerate the discipline of the inane classroom, are labeled as mentally challenged in one way or another and are even often medicated, while the kids who are most damaged are treated as healthy.

Let's turn now to the second question that I posed: "Who are the mavericks?" In other words, who are the ones who are suitable, who can be successfully reclaimed? How have they managed to maintain their individuality, to retain some initiative, to somehow be in touch with their evolutionary nature? We've been asking these questions for thirty years, but the fact is, we don't have a clue to the answer. People ask it all the time. Why me and not my brother? Why you and not somebody else? We know it's not a question of class, because we have people from every class, every economic level. We have people from every religion. We have people from every cultural background. It's funny to hear the assumptions that other people make about who comes to this school. People say, "You probably have a lot of university people, because this is something that has been given so much thought." We say, "No, we don't do too well with those." We have some, but not too many. They say, "You must have people who are left of center politically because it sounds like a leftist-radical place – empowerment of the common man and all that." We have some, but we also have a lot of very non-left people here, a lot of old Yankee conservatives. They make all these assumptions about the kind of people who they're sure populate this school. The fact of the matter is, we haven't been able to make any generalizations at all. We don't know.

In every case, it seems to be an accident of individual genetics and personal background that brings each member of this strange collection of people to Sudbury Valley. I mean that quite literally. When we started working on the school in 1966, it was the same kind of phenomenon. We hoisted our flag and declared, "We're starting this kind of school." We sent out mass mailings hither and yon, and people just appeared from all kinds of different places, people we never knew. It wasn't our friends. It wasn't some group that had a lot in common with each other. We didn't know any of the founders. Most of the founders didn't know each other. They just came; where, how, and why has been a puzzle ever since.

Let me conclude by addressing the question of why Sudbury Valley isn't for everyone. The answer is that Sudbury Valley *is* for everybody in a stable, self-sustaining, post-industrial society where everyone is on board. It's not a special kind of school for special kids. It's really a place where people in their natural state can flourish. But because there are so many real disabilities that exist during this transition period in history, the full benefits of the school are basically available only to mavericks, to those who haven't sustained a lot of damage that's made them incapable of living in their evolutionary natural state. To be sure, a lot of people who have sustained some damage, if they stick it out, seem to get considerable benefit from being here. That's more than a little consolation. In a sense, they get a glimpse of the Promised Land, like Moses on the top of Mount Nebo, just before he died. He looked at the Promised Land and then he died. They get a view of what the school is about, and then they move on.

We often hear that from former students, even those who have been here a very short time. It's our hope that as these benefits become more widely recognized and accepted, the whole culture will adapt, and the disabilities and damages will fade away.

There is a wealth of published material explaining the fundamental ideas upon which the Sudbury model is based, the product of several decades of experience and thought. The Sudbury Valley School Press offers a list of all the items currently available. Included are such classics as *Free At Last, The Sudbury Valley School Experience, Kingdom of Childhood, Reflections on the Sudbury School Concept, Worlds in Creation, A New Look at Schools,* and *Legacy of Trust.* The *Sudbury School Planning Kit* contains copies of virtually all of the available literature, tapes, etc., at a considerable discount.

For more information, contact The Sudbury Valley School Press, 2 Winch Street, Framingham, MA 01701. Phone: 508-877-3030; FAX: 508-788-0674.